Isla
Chronicles

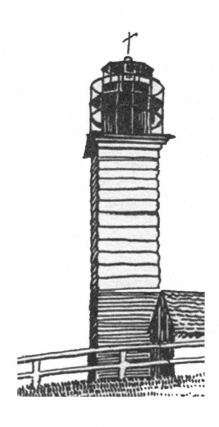

Stories from
Jamestown, Rhode Island

Island

Chronicles

Stories from
Jamestown, Rhode Island

Written and edited by
Rosemary Enright
and
Sue Maden

Published by the
Jamestown Historical Society
Jamestown, RI 02835

www.jamestownhistoricalsociety.org

Front cover: JHS A2006.061.001 (detail)
Back cover (top): Jamestown Windmill by John Price Wetherill (detail) courtesy of
Rosemary Enright
Back cover (bottom): JHS P2019.200.420 (postcard)

First published 2023

Manufactured in the United States

ISBN: 9798378330126

Table of Contents

Preface

Most of the essays in this collection are rooted in the period of immense and rapid growth that occurred in Jamestown between the introduction of the steam ferry to Newport in 1873 and Great Depression of the 1930s.

The island population fell slowly after the American Revolution until, in 1870, there were only 378 people living in Jamestown. The town was being drained of its young people, such as the Clarke brothers whom you will meet in "Those Clarke Women" (page 13), an essay about their daughters. Thomas H. Clarke went only as far away as Newport, while his brother David settled in South Carolina. Gustavus Adolphus Clarke (page 149) from the same extended family left the island with his widowed mother as a teenager.

Things began to turn around in 1873.

Economical and efficient steam-operated boats had been around for over 50 years. The steam ferry between Manhattan and Staten Island had begun in 1817. The floating palaces of the Fall River Line, which carried passengers from New York to Fall River with middle of the night stops in Newport, had been sailing past Jamestown since 1847.

Getting to and from Jamestown still depended on the wind. Since no one outside of Jamestown was interested in improving transportation to the island, the town itself put up 60 percent of the money to build a suitable ferry wharf and purchase a small steamboat, the *Jamestown*, the first of four ferryboats of that name.

The result was the beginning of Jamestown's era as a summer resort. By the turn of the century, the town's full-time population had tripled, there were accommodations for over 1,100 visitors at nine hotels and inns, Shoreby Hill had been laid out with 64 house plots, and summer cottages had sprung up all along Walcott Avenue and in the Dumplings. Conanicut Park at the far north end was a summer community all its own.

One of the inns was owned and operated by Hester and Emilie Tennant, profiled in "The Tennant Sisters" (page 27). Visitors, such as Mabel Brice Wheeler (page 23) and Eliza Hickey Newcomb Alexander (page 25), bought the cottages and came summer after summer to enjoy the island breezes.

The streets in the new plats had to have names. Their names ("Antham Street and Avenue B," page 45) and, sometimes, their renaming ("Narragansett Avenue or Ferry Road?" page 59) tell stories of their own.

The influx of summer residents brought new opportunities. The Peckhams, an old Jamestown family, moved from farming to hauling and horse trading ("The Peckhams: Father and Son," page 173). Members of Caswell family ("The Caswell Clan," page 161), another familiar Jamestown name, became artists, inventors, mechanics, and ferrymen.

The prosperity of the town attracted off-islanders to set up new businesses. J. Howard Bowen bought his inn and restaurant on the waterfront in 1928 ("The Bowen Brothers, page 153). A drugstore opened in 1930 ("Thomas E. Hunt, Jamestown's First Year-Round Druggist," page 157) .

Not all of these changes were greeted with enthusiasm by the intensely conservative townspeople, or indeed by the summer residents who wished to retain the rural charm that had attracted them to the island. In 1904, when the windmill on Windmill Hill was no longer profitable and had fallen into disrepair, the visitors and the residents worked together in a successful effort to save it ("Jamestown's First Preservation Effort: The Jamestown Windmill," page 103). Protection of the Conanicut Battery was first argued as early as 1915, although the intervening World Wars made deliberate action unnecessary until the 21st century ("Preserving the 1776 Conanicut Battery," page 117).

The growing business community gave rise to new organizations to foster group action. The organizations had been unnecessary in the close-knit agricultural community of the early 19th century, and most of these were formed after the Great Depression. The Jamestown Board of Trade (page 127), however, started in 1929 and quickly became a conduit for action to offset the effects of the depression.

Most of the essays in this collection originally appeared in *The Jamestown Press* as part of a series of monthly articles about the town and its past inhabitants that began in 2012. The three essays in "Touring Jamestown before the Bridges" (beginning on page 63) are from a different time and by different authors. They were written in 1893, 1902, and 1928, respectively, by individuals who lived in or visited Jamestown at that time. They present a contemporary view of Jamestown in the Resort Era.

ACKNOWLEDGMENTS

Many people were instrumental in getting this book to press. The members of the Jamestown Historical Society, especially the Collections Committee, provided expertise as the essays were developed. The staff of the Town of Jamestown willingly helped with research. Publisher Robert Berczuk and editor Tim Riel at *The Jamestown Press* printed the original versions of the essays. Joyce Allphin read every word.

Thank you all for your help.

Noteworthy but Seldom Noted: Some Jamestown Women

INTRODUCTION

Women in 19th and early 20th century – at least white middle- and upper-class women – were expected to marry and to confine themselves to the private sphere of home and family. If they did not marry, they continued to live with their parents and/or siblings. If that was not an option, they shared a home with a female friend. A woman living alone was assumed to be lacking in virtue.

Married women did not work. In 1890, only 4.5 percent of all married women were gainfully employed. Job opportunities for single women were limited, both by convention and by law. Those who did join the labor force were usually paid considerably less than their male co-workers. For example, in

Rhode Island in 1875 female teachers were paid an average of 54 percent of the salary of their male counterparts.

The "Cult of Domesticity," as it was dubbed by later historians, did not mean that women should be weak or uneducated. As *Godey's Lady's Book*, one of the most widely circulated women's magazines of the era, explained: "The companion of man should be able thoroughly to sympathize with him — her intellect should be as well developed as his. We do not believe in the mental inequality of the sexes; we believe that the man and the woman have each a work to do, for which they are specially qualified, and in which they are called to excel. Though the work is not the same, it is equally noble, and demands an equal exercise of capacity."

This ideal woman provided the moral compass for the family and, by extension, the nation. At a local level, she involved herself in the philanthropic and educational activities of the community.

Jamestown women in general conformed to society's norms. Within those constraints they moved forcefully.

THOSE CLARKE WOMEN

Joseph Clarke (1618-1694) was one of the original purchasers of Conanicut Island. He was the younger brother of John Clarke, the man who negotiated the Rhode Island charter signed by King Charles II in 1663 giving unprecedented religious freedom to the colony.

Among his descendants were six Clarke women born in the mid-19th century.

The cousins were the daughters of two brothers – David Otis Clarke (1827-1917) and Thomas Hartwell Clarke (1834-1919). The brothers were born in Jamestown. As young men, both brothers left the island, which at the time was an agricultural backwater of fewer than 400 people.

JHS P1976.115

Thomas Hartwell Clarke, father of Lena, Mary, Clara, and Jennie Clarke.

David Otis Clarke traveled to South Carolina, where he purchased a plantation. The family lived in South Carolina during the Civil War, then moved to Florida before coming back to Jamestown.

13

Thomas Hartwell Clarke became a teacher and later superintendent of schools in Newport. He brought the family back to Jamestown in 1882 and served as superintendent of schools here. The Thomas H. Clarke School, built in 1923 on the site of the current Jamestown Philomenian Library, was named in his honor.

All six Clarke female cousins were interested in Jamestown's history and five of the six spent most of their adult lives on the island.

Flora Clarke Weeden

The eldest of the cousins by more than 10 years was Flora (1853-1939). Flora grew up in the ante-bellum and Civil War South, coming to Jamestown with her family in her teens. In her mid 30s, she married Charles E. Weeden, the descendant of another original settler of Conanicut Island. Together they managed Prospect House, a small inn on Green Lane, and later the 110-room Hotel Thorndike on Conanicus Avenue where BankNewport is now.

JHS P2009.005.002

Charles E. Weeden.

Despite her busy life as an innkeeper, Flora helped found the Jamestown Historical Society and was its first Vice President. She later served as treasurer. She was for

14

many years a member of the Jamestown Philomenian Library Board of Trustees.

Elizabeth Clarke Helmick

Flora's younger sister by 13 years, Elizabeth Clarke Helmick (1866-1951), was the only one of the cousins to travel much beyond the shores of Conanicut Island. She married Lieutenant, later

JHS P2017.022.001

Prospect House, the inn managed by Flora Clarke Weeden and her husband Charles.

Major General, Eli A. Helmick, and when possible followed him to his posts. When she was unable to be with him, Jamestown was her home.

In 1931, Elizabeth and her cousin Lena wrote the first full history of Jamestown, which was published in a series of 16 articles in the *Newport Daily News*.

Elizabeth did not confine her historic interests to Jamestown. During her husband's assignment as a Military Science faculty member at

Courtesy of Pi Beta Phi

Elizabeth Clarke Helmick.

Hillsdale College in Michigan, she enrolled at the college and was inducted into the Pi Beta Phi women's fraternity. In 1915, she published a complete history of the fraternity, which had been founded in 1867 and was the first national secret college society of women to be modeled after the men's Greek-letter fraternity.

She was chair of the Pi Beta Phi committee that established a settlement school (now Arrowmont School of Arts and Crafts) in Gatlinburg, Tennessee, in 1912. The school provided the only public education for children in the area until the early 1940s.

She was later national adjutant general of the Daughters of the American Revolution.

Lena Clarke

Lena Clarke (1867-1955) was the eldest of the four daughters of Thomas Hartwell Clarke.

When the family moved from Newport to Jamestown in Lena's teens, Lena quit school, perhaps because the high school was off-island and the only way to get there was to take the ferry across the East Passage each day. In her mid-20s, however, she took summer courses at Harvard – probably under the

JHS P1982J.026
Lena Clarke on the steps of the Thomas H. Clarke School about 1930.

16

auspices of the Harvard annex that in 1894 was chartered as Radcliffe College.

She returned to Jamestown and, in 1895, began teaching in the "little schoolhouse" on Southwest Avenue. The building was later moved to Narragansett Avenue and was for many years the town library. It is now the Jamestown Museum. Her students in the one-room building were children who today would be in the lower grades. At the time there were no separate grades and Lena was expected to help each child proceed at their own pace.

Lena was a charter member and the first President of the Jamestown Historical Society, which was founded in 1912.

Lena was also the first contributor to the historical society's photography collection. In 1920, she and her friend Maude

JHS P1982.034

Lena Clarke (far right) and her sister Mary Clarke Hammond (sitting on running board) with other members of the Hammond family.

17

Stevens toured the island, taking snapshots of old houses and buildings such as the town animal pound. Lena put the photographs in an album with short write ups about the location and ownership of the buildings. She donated the album to the society and followed up with a monograph "Some Old Houses in Jamestown" and a more detailed description of Captain Thomas Paine's *Cajacet* on East Shore Road, one of the oldest houses on the island.

Jamestown was incorporated in 1678. The 350th anniversary of the town in 1928 was cause for a huge celebration that included an eight-episode pageant depicting some of the events in Jamestown history from the settlement to the Revolution. Lena collaborated with Walter Leon Watson on the scripts for the pageant and on a 23-page history of the town that was included in the souvenir program. Three years later, she and her cousin Elizabeth expanded the essay into the 16-part "History of Jamestown" for the *Newport Daily News*.

Throughout her adult life, Lena lived in the house on Narragansett Avenue across from the fire station that her father had bought when he brought the family to Jamestown in 1882. As was traditional, the women in the family lived at home until they married or died. The Clarke household included Lena's parents, her two unmarried sisters Clara and Jennie, and until their marriages her brothers Charles and William and sister Mary. After her mother's death in 1897, Lena took over the responsibility of the household, caring for her father until his death in 1919.

When she retired from teaching in 1938, Lena had taught three generations of Jamestown children and was principal of the Carr School, the elementary school that stood on Clarke Street near Southwest Avenue.

Mary Clarke Hammond

Mary Clarke Hammond (1871-1948) taught kindergarten in Newport and was superintendent of Trinity Church Sunday School until her marriage to John E. Hammond in 1905. Hammond was a prosperous Jamestown farmer and the elected

JHS P2001.010

Mary Clarke Hammond.

Jamestown Town Clerk from 1932 to 1953. After her marriage – since at the time, it was considered unfitting for married women to teach – she joined with her sisters to expand intellectual opportunities in Jamestown.

For 15 years, Mary was the librarian at the Jamestown Philomenian Library, which after 1898 was housed in the one-room schoolhouse where her sister Lena had begun her teaching career.

In 1939, Mary wrote *History of Conanicut Grange No. 21* to commemorate the 50th anniversary of the Grange of the Patrons of Husbandry organization on the island. She organized and was president of the Jamestown Mother's Club, the forerunner of the present Parent Teacher Association.

JHS P1982.035

Jennie and Clara Clarke, sitting on a horse-drawn, two-wheeled hay rake at their sister Mary Hammond's farm.

She was also the historical society's librarian and curator and contributed to Lena and Elizabeth's 1931 history of the town.

JHS P1982C.016

Clara Clarke on the beach.

Clara Clarke

Clara Clarke (1878-1954) was the least active of the cousins. After graduating from Rhode Island School of Design, she lived with her two sisters Lena and Jennie and worked as a bookkeeper at the Jamestown Garage down the street. She was also assistant librarian at the Jamestown Philomenian Library under her sister Mary for 20 years.

Jennie Clarke

JHS P2017.009.004

Jennie Clarke.

Jennie Clarke (1880-1972) – whose given name was Sarah Jane, a name that was never used – was the youngest and longest lived of the sisters. She was a Jamestown telephone operator and manager of the telephone office on the island for 38 years.

These were the days when to make a telephone call, you picked up the receiver and spoke directly to the operator, asking to be connected to the desired number. The operators knew almost everything that went on in the town and were often the source of news about town events.

Many stories are told of an operator helping residents trying to connect with other residents. They would redirect calls to a different number because they knew the person being called was not at home, but visiting elsewhere on the island. An hysterical child would be calmed down while a parent was located.

Like her oldest sister, Jennie was fascinated by history – or at least by the making of history. From 1916 to 1950, she kept scrapbooks of news items about Jamestown. Ten of her scrapbooks, now in the Jamestown Historical Society collection, document 35 years of day-to-day life in Jamestown.

JHS P1982J.018

Jennie Clarke in front of the telephone office at Narragansett Avenue and Coronado Street. The policeman is identified only as "Rudolph."

MABEL BRICE WHEELER

Mabel Brice was born in Philadelphia in July 1877 and, like many young women of her social set, she seems to have done little of interest for the first 35 years of her life. She, her brother Charles, and sister Anna lived with their parents in her mother's family home in Philadelphia. In the 1890s and early 1900s, the family traveled to Jamestown for the summer, where they were members of the Conanicut Yacht Club and participated in the social activities of the summer visitors.

Mabel's younger sister and brother married in the first decade of the new century. Her father, Ephraim, died in 1909. Mabel and her mother began spending summers in Europe rather than Jamestown.

The two women were in Aix-les-Bains, France, in late July 1914 when the events that precipitated World War I erupted. For over two weeks their whereabouts were unknown as they made their way across France to the relative safety of England. Perhaps it was this experience as a refugee that excited Mabel's sympathy for the people – especially the Belgians – who were being displaced by the war.

After the German invasion of Belgium on August 3, 1914, the country suffered a severe food shortage. The tiny nation did not grow enough food to meet its own needs, and the occupying army was taking what there was. The civilian population faced imminent starvation.

On her return home, Mabel Brice joined the Belgian Relief Committee of the Emergency Aid of Philadelphia. The committee collected food, clothing, and money for the people of Belgium. Donations were forwarded to the refugees in England and France, to civilians in uninvaded Belgium, and through the Commission for Relief in Belgium to the people of occupied Belgium. Hospital supplies were sent to Belgian hospitals and convalescent homes in France and England.

Between October 1914 and February 1920, the Packing Committee, which Mabel chaired, packed 1,273 cases, totaling 43 tons in bulk and containing 889,833 articles valued at $405,193.00 (approximately $6,000,000 in 2023). All cases arrived safely at their destinations except three cases lost to a submarine torpedo attack and two cases lost when a dock at Calais was bombed.

The work of the Belgian Relief Committee did not go unnoticed. On October 27, 1919, their Majesties King Albert and Queen Elisabeth of the Belgians awarded Mabel Brice the Order of Elisabeth, a medal given to women for religious and charitable work.

In 1920, at the age of 42, Mabel married Walter S. Wheeler, also of Philadelphia. Newspapers described Wheeler as a "clubman and big game hunter," whose observations on his hunting expeditions led to his election to the Royal Geographical Society of London. The newlyweds made their home with Mabel's mother in the house where she had grown up.

As Mrs. Wheeler, Mabel led the life typical of a Philadelphia society matron of the time. She became Vice-President and Treasurer of the Emergency Aid of Philadelphia organi-

JHS 2008.050.001

Portrait of Mabel Brice, later Wheeler, by Adolphe Borie (1977-1934), a well-known American portrait artist.

Courtesy of wikimedia.org
**Order of Queen Elis-
abeth, awarded to
Mabel Brice in 1919.**

zation, which after the end of the war focused its attention on combating the influenza and polio epidemics and alleviating the effects of post-war unemployment. She served on the board of governors of the Swedish-American Society, Oncologic Hospital, and the Historical Society of Pennsylvania as well as on committees of other charitable organizations.

The visits to Jamestown continued although with less frequency and shorter duration. Her husband died in 1936, and her brother, Charles, passed away in 1951. In 1952, she and her widowed sister-in-law bought the house at 4 Walcott Avenue.

The house had been one of three rental units built around 1900 by the Horgan family as part of the Thorndike Hotel complex. Until 1942, the Horgan property extended from Old Walcott to the East Passage. The roadway in front of the houses originally ran only to the John Price Wetherill cottage. During World War II, the military redesigned Walcott to be a continuation of Conanicus Avenue and go between the cottages and the water. The new layout of Walcott changed the character of the Horgan properties and in 1946, the Horgans subdivided the property and sold the houses.

Mabel visited Jamestown occasionally until her death in 1965 at age 88. She bequeathed her house to St. Matthew's Episcopal Church and its contents to the Jamestown Historical Society..

THE TENNANT SISTERS

Born in Jamestown in 1873 and 1874 respectively, Hester and Emilie Tennant grew up in the family home on Narragansett Avenue. They went to Jamestown's South School in the days of one-room schoolhouses when the Jamestown schools educated local students to the equivalent of the ninth grade.

While some of their classmates went on to Rogers High School in Newport, the two girls did not. After their mother's

JHS P1968.153

Students and teachers at Jamestown's South School in 1885. The school was on Southwest Avenue near Mackerel Cove.

death in 1901, they cared for their father, who in his late 60s was still working as a painter and as custodian at the new Carr School, built in 1898.

Early in the 1900s, romance entered Emilie's life in the person of Hermannus Klaassens. Klaassens had been born in Holland in 1873 but had come to the United States at the age of 6 and became a citizen in 1903. In 1900, he enlisted in the U.S. Army and served at Fort Wetherill in Jamestown and at Fort Kearney in Saunderstown. After his discharge, he decided to stay in Rhode Island and joined the Clarence A. Hammett real estate and insurance firm in Newport.

How Emilie and Hermannus met is unknown. Perhaps it was while he was stationed in Jamestown in 1903 and 1904. Perhaps Hammett's Newport Co-operative Association for Saving and Building brought them together, since Jamestown

JHS P2014.001.004

"The Cedars," the Tennant sisters boardinghouse at 49 (now 59) Narragansett Avenue.

had no bank and the sisters were beginning to take in boarders at the house at 49 Narragansett Avenue (now #59).

The couple married in June 1906. Klaassens continued working in Newport and, when his employer died in 1907, he and Anna Butler, who had also worked for Hammett companies, took over the real estate and insurance business. In March 1908, Klaassens was elected secretary of the Newport Co-operative Association.

Less than a year later, on February 20, 1909, Klaassens left for Fall River with $4,000 of the Newport Co-operative's funds and disappeared. The police searched for him for months, but no trace was found.

In the aftermath of the scandal, the sisters went back to living the life with which they were familiar – with Emilie perhaps trying to forget her five years of romance and excitement. For the next 10 years, they lived quietly, renting rooms in the large Narragansett Avenue house to boarders and taking care of their aging father.

Hester, who seems in general to be the more adventurous of the two, got involved in Town politics. She was elected Town Auditor in 1921 on a ticket that advertised "VOTE for this ticket to bar all CATHOLICS from office."

That same year, their father died, and the sisters

JHS P2004M.149

The house at 4 Grinnell Street that the Tennant sisters built in 1928.

29

moved to an apartment on Lawn Avenue, treating the Narragansett Avenue house as a boutique hotel. They bought the property across the street at the corner of Narragansett Avenue and Grinnell Street and, in 1928, built a six-room cottage for themselves. [The house was demolished in 2018 for the fire station expansion.]

The only Klaassens issue remaining was his will. Until he could be declared dead, the will could not be probated. Although his death could have been assumed in 1917 after he had not been heard from for seven years, it wasn't until 1938, when Klaassens had been gone almost 30 years, that his will was filed for probate. Emilie was the chief beneficiary, with small bequests going to members of his family in Amsterdam and $50 to Hester. The value of the estate is unknown.

That final remembrance of the short-lived marriage out of the way, the sisters settled once again into the routine of boardinghouse keepers. When World War II began, the military flooded the island keeping the boardinghouse busy. In addition, Hester got a job working at the Torpedo Station in Newport – her first ever off-island job.

After the war, the sisters – now in their 70s – moved back to the Narragansett Avenue house and Emilie died there in 1957. Hester moved to the Harbor View Nursing Home on Conanicus Avenue where she died three years later. She had written ten years earlier that her funeral would take place on May 9. She missed the date by a month, dying on June 11.

Ellen Tucker Cottrell

Ellen Tucker, the eldest child of Pardon and Sarah Waite Tucker, was born three days after Christmas in 1847 at the Hutchinson farm on North Road.

Ellen's early schooling was in the Jamestown schools, but when she was in her mid-teens, her father sent her away to Wheaton Seminary, now Wheaton College, in Norton, Massachusetts. Wheaton was one of the many female seminaries that were founded in the mid-19th century to instruct women in subjects, like mathematics, literature, and languages, that until that time had been the realm of the male-only univer-

JHS P1984.206

Ellen's parents Sarah Waite and Pardon Tucker.

sities. The seminaries also served as finishing schools that inculcated a standard of manners and decorum that defined how a woman could properly use her new-found knowledge.

Ellen Tucker married Frederick Northrup Cottrell in February 1867, when she was 19 years old. Her new home was the 400-plus-acre Cottrell Farm that extended from Hamilton Avenue south, surrounded on three sides by the waters of Narragansett Bay and Mackerel Cove.

Over the next 10 years, the couple had four children – Charles in 1869, Martha in 1871, Benjamin in 1873, and Alice in 1878.

Ellen's husband Frederick did not want to be a farmer. He dreamed of changing the island from an agricultural backwater to a summer tourist destination. He was one of the town fathers who formed the steam ferry company in 1872 and served as the company's treasurer. He represented the town in the General Assembly for eight years. In 1874, he formed the Ocean Highlands Company with himself as president, platted Highland Drive, and began to sell his land in the southern Dumplings as house lots.

JHS P1976.106

Ellen's husband Frederick Cottrell.

He died at age 49 in 1884. Ellen was only 36 and their youngest child was five.

According to Ellen's great-grandson Harry Burn, after Frederick N. Cottrell's estate was settled in 1886, Ellen Tucker gave each of their two sons, Charles and Benjamin, the sum of $15,000, with the admonition "This is your inheritance. When it's gone, don't come back for more." Their inheritance would be about $400,000 in today's dollars, and if the story is true, the young men made good use of their funds. Charles became a successful Boston lawyer. Benjamin got a Mechanical Engineering degree from Cornell University, did well in business, and bought Fox Hill Farm for his retirement.

Soon after her husband's death, Ellen left the farm. She built a house near her parents' house on

JHS P1984.210

Ellen Tucker Cottrell.

33

Brook Street and continued the process of subdividing the old Cottrell Farm.

The young widow became active in town affairs – often in defense of moral rectitude. She first appears in town records in 1888 when William C. Watson petitioned the Town Council for a license to operate a billiard table. Ellen Cottrell protested and presented a petition signed by 112 people, whom she affirmed were "taxpayers and others representing property to the amount of a half million dollars." In her opposition statements, Ellen drew a picture of a town riddled with disreputable establishments.

She did not prevail, and the license was granted.

The defeat did not dampen her determination to make Jamestown a model community. She was active in Central Baptist Church and served on the school committee. In 1907, she expanded her horizons to the state and was appointed by the Rhode Island Senate as a member of the board of female visitors to institutions where women were confined. In 1909, she was one of 32 women from the Women's Christian Temperance Union of Jamestown to petition the Town Council "to suppress the unlawful sale and dispersing of liquor in the town."

Although Ellen spent most of her life in Jamestown and nearby New England, in 1903 – the year after her father's death – she and her younger daughter Alice traveled to Europe.

From her mid-70s until her death in 1929 at 82 years of age, Ellen was an invalid, confined to her home on Brook Street.

ELIZA HICKEY NEWCOMB ALEXANDER

Eliza Hickey Newcomb was a Southern belle, born in Baton Rouge, Louisiana, in 1838. At 27, she married Junius Brutus Alexander, a New York investment banker 24 years her senior.

It was a stormy marriage.

Eliza and Junius had different opinions about the proper activities of a married woman. Eliza was an accomplished artist and nature writer who published several books of nature studies and whose landscapes were exhibited at the National Academy of Design. Junius disparaged and attempted to forbid her involvement in these "frivolous pursuits."

In addition, his children from his first marriage did not approve of his marrying a woman closer to their age than to his own and let the couple know their unhappiness.

The births of two children – Junius Jr. in 1867 and Maria Louisa in 1869 – seem to have fueled rather than reduced their disagreements.

Courtesy of New York City Historic District Council
Effingham House, the Alexander's home on Staten Island.

At least some of the arguments were about money. In 1873, after a brief separation, their reconciliation agreement included her promise that she would not run up bills.

The reconciliation lasted only a month. This time Junius seems to have been more interested in getting his children back than in his wife's return. He obtained a court order that she was to return the children to his house. Rather than obey the court order, Eliza took the children to Europe where they remained for seven years.

After a second attempt at reconciliation, Eliza and Junius signed a legal separation agreement in 1883 in which she retained custody of the children – now in their early teens – and Junius guaranteed her the income from $75,000 (about $1,900,000 in 2023 money) for the family's support.

During the ten years following the separation, Eliza and her children lived unexceptional lives. Junius Jr. attended Harvard, class of 1890. That June, he married Effie Shaw Emmons and the young couple moved to Sedro, Washington. Maria Louisa married Boston executive Reuben Francis Richards in 1891.

Eliza herself began her 20 years as a Jamestown summer cottager. Soon after her visit in 1889, she expressed interest in buying a permanent residence. Perhaps constrained by limited finances, she continued to rent.

Following a visit to her son and his bride in 1892, she sponsored an art reception and musicale at the Bay View Hotel to raise money to build a hospital in her son's new West Coast hometown.

The death of Eliza's estranged husband in 1893 initiated a whole new drama. There was no will. The six surviving children of his first marriage claimed the whole $1,000,000 plus estate. They argued that in accepting the $75,000 separation agreement,

JHS P1996.005

The steam yacht *Ripple* in front of Charles Wharton's *Braecleugh*.

which included a codicil giving each of her two children $25,000 and the residual of the $75,000, Eliza waived her and her children's right to inherit.

The courts disagreed. "[Mrs. Alexander] took her chances as to probability that her husband would dispose of his personal estate by will and would have omitted her name completely from such a document," wrote New York Supreme Court Justice George C. Barrett in 1895. "In no possible view of the law could Mrs. Alexander or her children be deprived of their rights merely because they accepted their share of the provision made for them in the deed of separation."

With her one-third of her husband's estate, Eliza bought Charles Wharton's steam yacht *Ripple* and two properties in Jamestown. *Hill Crest* at 53 Coronado Street

JHS P1965.133

Hill Crest.

JHS P1968.036
Grey Ledge.

in the village was a six bedroom house that had been built by Isaac P. Carr only a few years earlier. The second property, one and half acres in the recently platted development of Ocean View on South Beavertail Farm, was an empty field.

She hired Philadelphia architect Wilson Eyre Jr. to design a cottage overlooking the East Passage about 500 yards north of Beavertail Light. Eyre placed the cottage at the water's edge with the southeasterly porch partially supported by posts dug into the slope to the rocky shore. A large stone archway bisecting the first floor served as both porte-cochère and terrace protected from the southerly winds. The second story of the shingled cottage nestled beneath a hip roof with dormers on each side.

The house was called *Grey Ledge*.

Eliza continued to visit Jamestown for several years using both houses. She was in her late 60s and ill when in 1908 she allowed her sister Louisa Roberta Wilmerding to turn *Grey Ledge* into a tea house. Eliza died in 1912. After that the tea house was open sporadically until the mid-1920s when her children sold the house and it became again a private home.

Grey Ledge was severely damaged in the 1938 Hurricane and burned down in 1942 soon after the area was acquired by the Federal government for Fort Burnside.

WOMEN IN OUR POST OFFICE

The first post office in Jamestown was established in 1847. At the time, women were less than one percent of federal Postmasters, and the Postmaster's salary was a percentage of the stamps sold. Mail was not delivered door-to-door; it was held by the Postmaster for pick up. The post office moved from place to place, usually in the home or business of the Postmaster. In Jamestown, with a tiny population of under 400 where everybody knew everybody, this informal postal service worked well.

Twenty-five years later, with the introduction of the steam ferry to Newport, things changed. The summer population mushroomed. The year-round population grew to support the new resort economy.

Annie Gardner Littlefield

In 1875, two years after the introduction of the steam ferry, Jamestown's first woman Postmaster, Annie Gardner Littlefield (1851-1924), was appointed. Annie was the daughter

JHS P1976.102

Annie Gardner Littlefield.

39

of Captain Stephen Gardner, the first captain of the James-town-Newport steam ferry. During the 1870s, Captain Gard-ner and his wife Sarah also operated a boardinghouse/hotel on Narragansett Avenue, and in 1883 they built the Gardner House, a summer hotel on the lot where the Recreation Center now stands.

Annie married Nathaniel Littlefield in the early 1870s and soon after the birth of their only son in 1875, the couple moved in with her parents to help run the hotel. They continued to be involved in the growing hospitality industry on James-town throughout their lives.

This ability to house the post office in a building that was open to the public, as well as her father's influence and the supportive presence of her husband and mother, probably helped Annie, who was only 24 years old and whose son was still an infant, to win this federal patronage position usually awarded in deference to power, influence, and race.

Mary Jane Clarke Watson

Annie held the Postmaster position for five years. She was followed by the only other woman ever to hold the office in Jamestown: Mary Jane Clarke Watson (1823-1888).

Mary Jane Clarke was the eldest of the nine children of David Wright and Sarah Munroe Clarke and a descendant of Joseph Clarke, one of the purchasers of Conanicut Island from the Narragansett in 1658. In 1847, she married John Eldred Watson of equally distinguished Jamestown lineage. The couple lived on Prospect Hill on Beavertail where Mary gave birth to eight children, two of whom died at a young age.

John E. – the "E." was always used with his name to distinguish him from his cousin John J. Watson – had been elected Town Clerk in 1844 and was re-elected every year until his death. He ran the Town Clerk's office out of his grocery store on Ferry Road, now Narragansett Avenue, and when Mary was appointed Postmaster in 1880, the post office also moved to Watson's grocery.

JHS P1976.127

Mary Jane Clarke Watson.

John E. died in 1882. The Jamestown Town Council appointed his son, John E. Watson Jr., to finish his father's term as Town Clerk with the general understanding that Mary would continue to fill the duties since, as Mary's obituary said, "she [being a woman] was unable to hold the office herself." Until her death in 1888, Mary Watson served as Postmaster and, except for a two-year period when their cousin John J. Watson was elected, as unofficial Town Clerk with her son.

Edith Caswell Richardson

Around the turn of the century, mail service in Jamestown changed to be similar to today's service, with a dedicated post office building and house-to-house delivery. Among the early mail carriers was Edith Caswell Richardson (1901-1994).

Edith Caswell was born in Jamestown and graduated from Jamestown's Carr School in 1914. In her 20s, she married Alfred V. Richardson. Their descendants still live in Jamestown.

Edith was a teenager when she went to work for the Jamestown post office in 1917 and was one of the first female rural mail carriers in the country. Until the mid-1930s, she traveled by horse and buggy in summer and by horse and sleigh in winter to deliver mail along Jamestown's Rural Free Delivery (RFD) route 1, which had been started about 1906.

JHS P2013.007.005
Edith Caswell Richardson.

Other Jamestown women have worked in the post office over the years: Ruth Browning Magill, Kathryn Spry Zweir, Jayne Chesbro Clarke, Eileen Blanchette Parfitt, and most recently Linda Armbrust Warner. Linda retired from the post office in 2000 after 31 years delivering mail along a rural delivery route of about 350 houses.

Jamestown Street Names

INTRODUCTION

When Joshua Fisher drew his map of Jamestown in 1658, he drew a road running straight north-south from the town almost to the north end of the island, without regard for the creek and marsh across which a bridge was finally built in 1729. A second road ran southwest out of town to Mackerel Cove as it does today. He did not name these roads North Road and Southwest Avenue, although how they got their names is obvious.

There are only a few east-west roads on Fisher's map. Over the years, these roads acquired the names of the farms they serviced. Carr Lane runs by the old Carr Homestead, built in its current configuration at the time of the American Revolution although an earlier structure certainly existed on the spot. Eldred Avenue went to the farm from which in 1775

John Eldred harassed the British revenuers with his one-gun battery. The Weedens lived on the family farm on the south side of Weeden Lane from the founding of the town until 1924.

The transformation of Jamestown from a farming community to a resort in the late 19th century led to a spate of new developments with new roads. Most of the platted developments followed some sort of naming scheme, although the earliest – the Mullins plat in Conanicut Park – with over 60 streets to name does not follow a consistent pattern.

The earliest in-town plat was Ferry Meadow, just south of East Ferry. Laid out in 1872, the street names – Union, Lincoln, Friendship – reflect the recently ended Civil War.

The group from St. Louis that established Shoreby Hill in 1898 chose to name several of their roads after popular 19th century New England writers – [Henry Wadsworth] Longfellow (1807-1882), [Ralph Waldo] Emerson (1803-1882), [John Greenleaf] Whittier (1807-1882) and [Nathaniel] Hawthorne (1804-1864). They paid further homage to Longfellow by naming three of the streets after the characters in his narrative poem "The Courtship of Miles Standish" – [John] Alden, [Miles] Standish, and Priscilla [Mullins]. The poem takes place in Plymouth, as another street is named.

The streets in the five plats of Jamestown Shores, although not all laid out at the same time, all reference the sea – ship types from Coracle to Frigate, ship parts from Garboard to Mast, and the occasional ship-related term, such as Nun, a type of buoy.

Some streets have more interesting Jamestown stories.

ANTHAM STREET AND AVENUE B

Antham Street is a one-block-long street between Clarke Street and Southwest Avenue. On early maps, this shortcut is called Avenue A. The land on either side of Avenue A was owned by Alvin H. Peckham and Louis Wayland Anthony.

Alvin H. Peckham came to Jamestown from Aquidneck Island in 1881 when he was in his mid-20s. He was a farmer and also owned a cart-ing business. Original-ly he used horses and heavy-duty carts to move materials to and from the ferries and around the island. As the new century approached, his transports changed to gasoline-powered trucks. He also built and owned a small inn, Harmony Villa, on Union Street.

JHS P2017.101.001

Alvin H. Peckham, in 1897 when he was Master of the Conanicut Grange.

Louis W. Anthony, five years younger than Peckham, lived almost his whole life in town. At the height of James-

45

JHS P2013.105.002

Louis W. Anthony at the height of his career in the 1920s.

town's building boom in the early 20th century, he was one of the town's busiest architect/builders, designing and constructing many of the smaller homes, especially in the village.

In 1898, Anthony and Peckham each deeded 15 feet of their property as a private road to service their farms. Five years later, the two men teamed up to found Jamestown's first lumber yard. Peckham hauled timber from a woodland that the two men bought in Canaan, New Hampshire. He stored it on his lot on Cole Street, possibly using the new road to bring the lumber to the lot. Both men used the lumber in their construction projects.

When they named their road, the men used a portmanteau of their surnames – the first three letters of Anthony and the last three letters of Peckham – to create the street name. So, no, Antham is not a misspelling of "anthem," but the playful conceit of two businessmen wanting equal billing on their mutually created lane.

The road was accepted as a public right-of-way in 1918.

Over near the West Ferry, running north from Narragansett Avenue, is a block-long cul-de-sac called Avenue B – a strangely urban name for what is still a rustic lane.

The first mention of Avenue "B" in town records is in a deed in 1895 when Isaac Briggs sold four acres of West Ferry land to William Gill – possibly his grandson Willie, who was then in his early 20s – for "one dollar and other valuable considerations."

Briggs had purchased the land in 1871. At that time, the limits of the plot were described as "northerly and easterly on land of Thomas C. Watson, southerly on a highway [Narragansett Avenue, then called Ferry Road] and westerly by Narragansett Bay." In 1895, the eastern border of the prop-

JHS P1989.021

The Ferry House on the north side of Narragansett Avenue at West Ferry in the early 20th century. The ell was a waiting room and convenience store.

erty was Avenue B, probably shorthand for the path Briggs used to get to his shore-front property.

The man who gave his initial as the name of one of our streets was born in Newport on May 26, 1820. He went to sea at an early age on the whaler *Fanny Fern*. Later he sailed out of Newport in command of schooners engaged in the West Indies and Gulf of Mexico trade. He twice lost his ship to sudden storms and drifted in an open boat until picked up. He served in the Civil War as captain of the transport schooner *Mary Mankin*.

Briggs was 50 years old and ready to do his sailing closer to home when he bought the property at West Ferry. The deed included the land and "a two-story dwelling, a cottage house . . . also one ferry boat, one sail boat, one row boat & tackling belonging to the same . . . with all the privileges and appurtenances including the 'west ferry' privileges."

The family – Briggs, his wife Elizabeth, his daughter Esther, Esther's husband John Gill, and until his death in 1873 Briggs' father, Gorton – lived in the ferry house. The

JHS P2018.107.001

The cottage on the West Ferry wharf where the boatman lived.

house also held the ferry waiting room in which tobacco, cigars, and other items for travelers were sold. Rooms could be rented by stranded travelers, although it was not a boarding house inviting people to stay for longer periods. Briggs farmed the land along the shore and operated the ferry. The ferry business was not brisk, and he sometimes rented out the sail and row boats or took visitors for sails.

As he grew older, Briggs hired other men to sail the ferry for him. The boatmen lived in the cottage house on the wharf.

A respected member of the community, the captain was elected Overseer of the Poor – the official in charge of social services for the town – four times in the 1880s and held other town offices.

He was also a trustee of Central Baptist Church and a Mason.

Captain Briggs was in his 70s when his water spaniel Tobey was featured in the *Newport Daily News*. According to the newspaper, Tobey was Captain Briggs' newsboy.

> *"He leaves his home at about 6 a.m., travels a mile to the ferry. Where he takes the boat for Newport. . . .Arriving in Newport he is furnished with the morning paper and sometimes a friend will place a bit of meat in a paper bag for the dog's breakfast. He then returns to the ferry with the newspaper and the bag, and, after arriving on the island proceeds to his home, his master receiving the morning paper shortly after 10 o'clock."*

During the summer, Tobey sometimes expanded his travels and took a trip on the ferry to Saunderstown after he delivered the paper.

Captain Isaac Bowen Briggs died at his West Ferry home on April 22, 1907. He was 87. Out of respect, the Town Council postponed the council meeting scheduled for the day of his funeral to the following week.

PIERCE AVENUE

Pierce Avenue near West Ferry is one of many Jamestown streets named after residents who changed the surrounding neighborhood.

Emma and Seth Pierce were in their fifties when they came to Jamestown from Providence where he had been a junk dealer and auctioneer. They first appear in Jamestown records in 1902, when Emma leased seven acres of "West Ferry Meadow" from Thomas Carr Watson.

Over the next several years she and her husband purchased more and more property at West Ferry. Watson sold them the land they had leased and three other parcels. Charles L. Bevins, the Jamestown architect who lived at Meadowsweet Farm between (now) Pierce and Maple avenues, sold them pieces of that farm. By 1906, the Pierces' consolidated holdings reached along Sheffield Cove from the West Passage to beyond Maple Avenue. At some points, the northern edge was Narragansett Avenue, but some properties – notably *Meadowsweet Farm* and *Thorncroft* – were still owned by others.

Seth Pierce built a barn, moved a stable and other buildings from Knowles Court to the West Ferry land (all of which was in his wife's name), and grazed cows and horses in the pastures. His farm auctions between 1907 and 1909 offered horses, cows, and pigs for sale and attracted local and off-island farmers.

In 1910, the Pierces, now both 60 years old, decided to make a change. They rented their property – now called "Shore Acres Farm" – to Aaron R. Richardson, and began to divide their time between Jamestown and Daytona, Florida.

JHS P2013.007.016

Aaron R. Richardson who leased the Pierce's Shore Acres Farm.

Two years later, the Pierces platted the eastern part of their property into house lots, laid out roads, and prepared to sell the lots at auction. The *Newport Daily News* advertisement on Friday, August 15, 1913, the day before the auction, extolled the desirable features of "Maple Grove." The plat sat "right in the very center of the island, midway Ferry to Ferry." Streets were already laid out and graded. Eight lots were located on the water, and three bungalows had already been built. The terms were "the easiest ever" – just $10 down, mortgages for up to 75 percent, no interest or taxes for one year.

"Lots on this plat sold last year have re-sold recently at twenty-five per-cent profit to the buyer. ... You can't lose, it is only a question of HOW MUCH will you make."

On the following Monday, the *Newport Daily News* reported a large crowd and a successful auction: The sale began with a 27,000-square-foot lot on Maple Avenue with a bungalow, garage, and a well of spring water which brought $2,795. Vacant lots sold for about $130 a piece. Many purchasers

JHS P2019.200.175

The cottage with a spring called the Fountain of Youth in Maple Grove.

bought more than one lot. The largest purchaser was Edward Littlefield who bought eight lots.

With the sale of the Maple Grove properties complete, Seth Pierce devoted his energies to selling the property along the West Passage. He called the new development "Bungalow Park."

Three streets running south from Narragansett Avenue – Congress, Marine, and Pierce – were laid out and graded. (In 1929, the Town Council changed Congress Street to Westwood Road at the request of the major property holders for a "less pretentious" name.) A fourth street along the water connecting Spring Street and Congress was planned. Late in 1914, the Pierces built a cottage for themselves on the street that bore their name.

A three-day auction began on Friday, July 31, 1914. By the end of the auction about one third of the plat had sold. The *Newport Daily News* commented "The prices brought by the lots were cheap for those who intend to build, and for the speculative purpose reasonable."

Seth Pierce's interest in Jamestown waned. Real estate ventures near his winter home in Florida captured his attention. "He is very enthusiastic over the future of the section and says more people than ever before are coming to Florida and Daytona from the state of Rhode Island this winter," the *New Smyrna Daily News* reported in November 1914.

Through 1915, the Bungalow Park lots sold slowly, and in mid-summer 1916, Pierce still had 30 lots on his hands. To get rid of them, he arranged a final auction. He told the *Newport Daily News*, "Now is the time to secure one of the most desirable seashore locations for present or future use, or for investment as I am positively closing out our real estate in Jamestown, at public auction, to the highest bidder, as I have a large interest in Florida, which will take my time and attentions."

At the auction on Saturday, August 19, 1916, everything was sold. While a few lots brought a reasonable price, the *Newport Journal* reported that many were sold for very little.

Emma Pierce sold the family's Pierce Avenue bungalow in 1917.

THE STREETS OF THE KNOWLES PLAT

The area of town tucked in between Upper Shore-by Hill and the Town Cemetery at the Four Corners was developed in the early 20th century and was known as the The land belonged to Adolphus C. Knowles, the owner and builder of the Bay View House Tower.

Knowles was an archi-tect/builder by occupa-tion. In addition to his hotel, he designed and built the Central Baptist Church and a number of homes on Shoreby Hill. He served as president of the Jamestown Town Council, acting Town Clerk, and General Trea-surer for Rhode Island. Although he was a direc-tor of the Jamestown & Newport Ferry Compa-ny, he also owned and operated an excursion boat, the *Sylvan Shore*, making trips between

JHS P2017.101.001

Adolphus C. Knowles in 1931, shortly after developing the Knowles plat.

Providence, Rocky Point, and Jamestown, providing ferry service between East Ferry and the Dumplings, and operating as a passenger ferry to Newport in opposition to the Jamestown & Newport Ferry Company boats.

Many streets in the plat are named for prominent Jamestown families of the time.

Douglas Street. The Douglass family in early Jamestown spelled its name with two "S"s. Several family members are buried in the Town Cemetery. Hannah Remington Douglass, who was the great granddaughter of John Martin, the only man killed when the British burned their way from East to West Ferry in December 1775, is buried next to the memorial stone for her husband Thomas who was drowned at sea in 1831.

The most prominent Douglass in late 19th century Jamestown was Thomas and Hannah's son John M. Douglass. A mason by trade, he was Jamestown's Assessor of Taxes for many years and represented the town in the state legislature as senator in 1860 and 1870 and as representative from 1847 to 1849 and from 1884 to 1890.

Fowler Street. The Fowlers were connected to the Douglass family. Hannah, John M. Douglass' eldest daughter, married Gilbert Fowler soon after the end of the Civil War. A native of Noank, Connecticut, Gilbert had served throughout the war in the First Connecticut cavalry. The couple had several daughters. The youngest, Dakota, died when she was six months old in 1880. Hannah died the following year, and the two are buried near each other in the Douglass plot in the town cemetery. After Hannah's death, Gilbert moved to

Newport where he worked as a painter. He died there 10 years later.

Luther Street. Albert W. Luther began his career as a shop-keeper in Newport. In the late 1880s, he realized the potential of Jamestown as a summer resort and moved to the island. With his brother-in-law Fred N. Cottrell and several other prominent Jamestowners, he formed the Ocean Highlands Company, which developed the Dumplings area. He was a director of the Jamestown & Newport Ferry Company, and for some years was its managing director. According to his 1907 obituary, Luther did "much, perhaps more than any other persons, in building up the claims of the town as a summer

JHS P1965.067

A.W. Luther's Real Estate office at East Ferry.

resort and was largely instrumental in inducing many of the present summer residents to purchase land and erect cottages there."

Swinburne Street. Swinburne Street is named for one of the families that lived on it. The Swinburnes came to Jamestown from Newport about the turn of the century. The father, George, was an early director of the Jamestown & Newport Ferry Company. His son John was part of the lumber and hardware firm of Swinburne and Peckham, and while working in a mill, he caught his hand in a tenoning machine and lost the four fingers of his left hand. John's daughter Elizabeth Swinburne-Champlin was a telephone operator for 50 years in the Jamestown office of the New England Telephone Company.

Harriet Street. Knowles did not give his own name to any of the streets; Knowles Court next to his hotel already honored the family. But the Knowles family was not entirely forgotten. Harriet Street is named for his youngest daughter, who married Private Edwin Anderson in November 1917, before he left to fight in the First World War. Anderson descendants and other relatives still live in Jamestown.

Not all streets in Knowles plat follow this naming pattern. Geography influenced the name of Valley Road, which runs through the lowest part of the plat, a distinction that was probably more visible at the time than it is today. Plymouth Road, an extension of a Shoreby Hill road, retained its name. Shady Lane, which is on the border between the Knowles plat and the George W. Carr farm, was originally Melrose Street, although there seems to have been no local association for that name.

NARRAGANSETT AVENUE OR FERRY ROAD?

In the 18th century, South County was a prosperous agricultural area, and Jamestown was a vital link between Newport and South County. Private ferries to Jamestown were available as early as 1675 when Captain Benjamin Church paid to have himself and some of his men carried from Newport to Saunderstown. John Carr's Newport-Jamestown ferry was licensed in 1700.

Where the ferries landed is less clear. On the east side, some landed north of town at Potter's Cove, and men and produce bound for the Narragansett country crossed the island on what was known for a time as North Ferry Road and later as Eldred Avenue. On the west side, some ferries from Saunderstown landed at Fox Hill.

JHS P1994.074

A view of Jamestown about 1830.

In 1709, the preeminence of the route from Dutch Island Harbor to the East Ferry wharf was established. That was the year that the road was designated a link in the branch of the Boston Post Road that ran from the Connecticut border to Narragansett and then to Newport on its way to Providence. Twenty-two lots were laid out along the north side of the road. Sixteen houses were built only to be destroyed by the British when they marched across the island, burning everything in their path, in December 1775.

Recovery from the depredations of the American Revolution was slow. Eighty-five years later in 1860, only nineteen houses lined the same route.

For 175 years, the tiny agricultural community seems not to have found it necessary to settle on a formal name for the one-mile long road between the East and West Passages. In town records, it is called alternatively the Post Road, the Post Highway, Ferry Road, and the road between the ferries.

When steam ferries to Newport were introduced in 1873, Jamestown entered an era of swift and lasting change. Farms were developed into communities of summer bungalows. New occupations – unrelated to the agricultural past – were introduced. A Town Hall was built. Civic pride suggested that the most traveled roadway in the community should have a permanent and important sounding name.

On May 18, 1884, 19 Jamestowners petitioned the Town Council to name the ferry road Narragansett Avenue

"Whereas Jamestown has become a popular Summer resort, many new buildings have been erected, and many new streets laid out and named, we the abutters of the principal thorough-fare of the Town leading from the East Ferry to the Narragansett ferry believe that said road should be named and that Narragansett Avenue would be an appropriate name."

The Council granted the petition. About that same time, Water Street along the eastern shore of the island became Conanicus Avenue.

Thirty years later, the question of the name came up again – this time prompted in part by members of the Jamestown Historical Society who wished to return to the more historic and descriptive designation.

In October 1915, a group – many of them summer people – petitioned the Town Council to change the name back from Narragansett Avenue to Ferry Road. The change was opposed by some of the most prominent businessmen in Jamestown, including John E. Watson, a grocer with a store on Narra-

JHS P2016.101.058

John E. Watson (above) and RADM Edward W. Taussig (below) took opposing sides in the debate to rename Narragansett Avenue Ferry Road.

JHS A2016.207.001

gansett Avenue, and Thomas Carr Watson, who represented Jamestown in the General Assembly for 22 years.

Despite his opposition to the name change, John E. Watson's invoices in 1915 read: "John E. Watson Dealer in Choice Family Groceries, Ferry Road." Obviously, there was still some schizophrenia about the 30-year-old name change.

Supporting the return to the old name were, among others, the town doctor Arthur M. Mendenhall and Rear Admiral Edward W. Taussig, (USN, RET), who had retired to Jamestown after 46 years in the navy. The *Electric Spark*, the newsletter of Dr. Bates's Sanitarium, reported that "William B. Franklin, whose great grandfather owned both ferries many years ago, spoke interestingly also in favor of the old name." Dr. William Lincoln Bates, president of the Jamestown Historical Society, read letters from members of the society and of the summer colony.

The Town Council voted in November, three to one, to retain the "new" name of Narragansett Avenue.

Touring Jamestown before the Bridges

INTRODUCTION

What did visitors see in Jamestown in the late 19th and early 20th centuries? Why did they come? Nothing answers those questions as fully as words written at the time. The three essays that follow are extracted from contemporary accounts.

"Conanicut Island, Conanicut Park and Jamestown" first appeared in *Pleasant Places in Rhode Island, and How to Reach Them,* an 1893 tour guide from the *Providence Journal.* Mariana M. Tallman, the author, traveled to summer tourist spots all around Narragansett Bay. Her impressions of each town are highly personal and meant to help the readers decide which resort would suit them best and, perhaps, to give the armchair traveler the impression of visiting each of them.

As the title implies, in the late 19th century, the tiny community of Conanicut Park at the north end of Conanicut Island was a separate village from the village of Jamestown. Conanicut Park had its own wharf at what is now Park Dock at the end of Broad Street. The ferries that stopped at the northern village brought visitors from Providence and points north.

The second essay, "A Community Made Prosperous in Spite of Itself," author unknown, appeared in the *Newport Journal* on September 13, 1902. It offers a unique view of the growth of tourism in Jamestown, emphasizing the town fathers' inability to recognize the advantages that such tourism brought.

The third essay, "The Heart of Narragansett Bay," was written as an advertising piece for the Conanicut Park Club project by Walter Leon Watson about 1928. Watson was a Carr descendant and well known in Jamestown for his historical writings about the town, which included "The House of Carr," written in 1926 about the history of the Carr family; the skits performed in 1928 in honor of the 250th anniversary of the incorporation of the town; and *The History of Jamestown on Conanicut Island in the State of Rhode Island*, published in 1949.

As far as could be discovered, the essay was never published.

Conanicut Island, Conanicut Park and Jamestown: 1893

by Mariana M. Tallman

As the one boat which deigns to pause at Conanicut Park sweeps in at the dock, a scent of bayberry from the wild slopes is first to welcome one. Next is the one hotel carriage, as one disembarks and the boat speeds down to Newport. It is well that the hotel is pleasant and well managed, for it is "Hobson's

JHS P1984.153

The Conanicut Park Hotel.

65

Choice;" but it is perched invitingly among the old trees up the slope, a pretty bit of color with its light gray walls and red turrets, and its pillared veranda green and shady with masses of woodbine.

Conanicut Park is emphatically a place of rest; its diversions, though many are of the mildest; its dissipations none. Its six mile length and one mile width have all the wayside delights of upland and ocean. Wild rose and iris, bayberry and elder-bloom crowd the northern meadow, and by and by a harvest of berries can be had for the gathering. Conanicut Island light, on the northeast shore, is a spot well worth a visit. Aside from the views to be gained from the lighthouse tower, Mr. H.W. Arnold, the keeper, a graduate from the Warwick Neck light, is the hero of the Conimicut Light disaster a few years ago – a victim of the ice-flood. He has been in charge here for five years and achieved the most admirable results. The yard of the pretty gray cottage from which the tower rises

JHS P2004.004.007

Conanicut Island North Light.

was then like the wilderness without a jungle of wild growth; it is now a neatly shaven velvet sward, dotted with flowers, and with the finest bed of nasturtiums possible to find in a long day's journey, shading through yellow and white and palest straw color to deepest crimson. Over the entire front of the house runs a great honeysuckle, a fragrant mass of yellow and white, and an uncommonly aspiring jessamine has ceased to become a shrub and run away up to the high eaves and the light tower.

The grounds about the hotel and even down to the water are reclaimed from their not unlovely wildness and form the real "park" which names the place. The station erected by the steamboat company, but sitting serenely above the bustle of the dock, is a pretty feature of the place, and the few quaint cottages are in excellent taste, that of Miss Jennie Lippitt, with grounds sloping to the water, being noticeably inviting, and

JHS P2002.001.001

Jenny Lippitt's "Stonewall Cottage."

JHS P1984.211

Charles Fletcher estate and yacht, 1886.

above it, also near the wild rocky shore, Charles Fletcher's spacious cottage, most imposing of all, with its round tower, clustering verandas and handsome lawns, closed in by a dense hedge of evergreens from the too wild blasts off the east winds. It has been the custom in past years for a party of gay girls, chaperoned by some not over-severe matron, to take possession of a Conanicut cottage for the summer and have their fill of innocent and healthy fun. It would be hard to say how many charming girls have learnt proficiency in swimming by a Conanicut season, stimulated by criticism and rivalry, and encouraged by calm water. Their only plaint is, amid the eulogies of beloved Conanicut, that "you can't spend anything there." Papa has neither to forward occasional checks during the daughter's stay, nor to settle sundry later and appalling bills. Conanicut has no store, no bazaar, not even an Indian tent and accompanying basket work. One cannot buy even a stamp there, for addresses read thus: "Miss

Blank, Conanicut Hotel, Conanicut Park, Newport, R.I." It is possible to run up a bill only with Mrs. Brown and the stable keeper, Mr. Paine. The stable is the one public luxury, and Mr. Paine furnishes saddle horses and various vehicles and drives the stranger all about the island, furnishing information and prancing steeds at the same time at most modest prices.

But the most notable and most praiseworthy feature of the place is the institution known as "Seaside Cottage," established now for fourteen years by the Providence Fountain Street Society – the admirable arrangement by which tired, ill or not over-wealthy city women and children may have a week or two of change and absolute rest at the small sum of $3 per week. Mrs. Wright, the matron, has charge for the fourth season, and her domain is a most delightful one.

Picture a quaint, low, old-fashioned gray farmhouse, with deep well and flat door stones, enlarged by ell and verandas,

JHS P2019.200.761

Seaside Cottage.

and nestled in the heart of a quiet old apple orchard, with huge, gnarled trunks, where the sun and shade frolic in the breezes that glow up from the salt waves, lapping the rocks almost at its foot. In a hollowed stone by the old well, the birds drink and bathe in a tiny pool, and twitter perpetually. This is Seaside Cottage, and a winding concrete walk leads down to the "children's cottage," under the same jurisdiction, but where the mothers with little folk abide, that the nervous and invalid be not disturbed at the larger house – a thoughtful provision which we would commend to the attention of hotel keepers generally. Mrs. White is assistant matron here. There are times where the matron has been called upon to entertain ninety in her entire fold.

Delightful as Conanicut is, it is not wholly pleasant to know that one cannot leave it when one is so disposed. The captain, the ticket agent and the starter all assured us that

JHS P2019.200.413a

Seaside Camp Children's Cottage.

***Eolus*. Built in 1864, the steamship ran between Newport and Wick-
ford from 1869 to 1894, with occasional stops at Conanicut Park.**

ferry boats to Wickford and Newport touched at the Park,
but they do not. The morning boat from Providence, and her
five o'clock return are the only landings, and the natives say
the ferry boats have not paused for weeks. The *Eolus* waxed
wroth since her encounter with the *Day Star,* and has conclud-
ed to let the latter vessel have her own way, it would seem.
What she might do if one were to stand at the dock's edge
in a commanding attitude and beckon in broad capitals, we
cannot say but just now a petition is circulating that the two
o'clock city-bound boat may stop there, as it ought.

To leave Conanicut otherwise means to enter Jamestown, and Mr. Paine's charioteer conducted us away from
the quiet north end of the island to the tumult of the south;
past Seaside Cottage again and the bit of an old graveyard
where lie the bones of that dead and gone habitant Paine,

JHS P2008.019.006

Champlin House.

over whom neighborhood gossip is just now exciting itself to settle whether he was in truth, as a revived tale has put it, a murdering, bloody pirate or a highly respected citizen and an ornament to the community. Past the old, old windmill, 150 years old, with its huge great arms, its revolving cap and its still staunch body, which yet earns its living like younger windmills, up the long slant of Freebody's Hill, the way adorned with youthful turkeylets roosting melancholy on the fence-tops; in sight of stately Newport and the white-winged fleet always hovering in the harbor, past the Champlin House and its opposite neighbor, the Bay Voyage, thus oddly named to commemorate its own trip across seas, and down at length into hustling Jamestown, lively already as in midsummer time, the imposing front of the gray and red Bay View blocking the way, and the docks below, bristling with sailboats and

JHS P1951.003

The ferryboat *Conanicut* at East Ferry about 1890.

lesser craft, and the towering hulk of the ferryboat *Conanicut*, swinging in from Newport. General bustle is in the air; and so is the Philadelphian and St. Louis accent, for these two cities populate the most of this growing summer town.

A long-standing mystery is solved. Now we know what becomes of all the boys and girls through the summer – they are in Jamestown. Newport claims the beaux, the Pier the belles and babies, Block Island the men and Watch Hill the nice old ladies – the silver-haired Aunt Serenas; but everywhere has there seemed sad lack of real genuine boys and girls till we landed at the Jamestown Wharf, and there they all were, as if the Hamelin piper had piped them all over the ferry from Newport. It is small wonder a new hotel has gone up since last season, and cottages without end, and that the sound of the plane and hammer is still heard in the land. Jamestown is a growth as rapid as any of the mushroom towns of the West.

JHS GN1978.026

The Jamestown Day parade passing the Thorndike Hotel in the late 1800s.

Six years ago, an old resident says, standing at the dock and looking into what is now the heart of the place, there were but eight houses to be counted – old settlers all, and readily to be distinguished now from their more modern neighbors, from the wee black hovel, with the lone pine tree near the landing, to the fine old Curry place, a bit up the north shore road, with its remarkable apple orchard that should have its home in the "Garden of the Gods," so weird, uncanny and gnarled are the giant sprawling limbs before feathering into soft foliage.

"Smith's" is another of the old places transformed now into a quaint, gray English Inn by the addition of an ell thrice its own size and looking like a younger sister of Greene's

Inn at the Pier. The houses that are not hotels are boarding houses unless they are cottages, and if they are cottages, they take lodgers with few exceptions. It is the liveliest place south of the daily shore resorts. To sit at one's window of an evening, albeit it is pretty well up in a crowded hotel where one is lucky to get a room at all – sitting here and listening to the voices of the night, predominant among them all is the confused babel of many voices like the roar of Broadway, and I do not mean the Broadway of Providence, deafening as that is, but New York.

"What is the chief attraction of Jamestown?" we asked an old settler.

"Well, it's the climate and the quiet," he answered. "Any number of Westerners come here who object to Newport and the Pier because they are not quiet."

Jamestown might, like the proprietor of a certain German spa, copy his advertisement with equal propriety, which reads: "People in search of absolute retirement and quiet are flocking here from every quarter of the globe."

Of the enthusiastic younger folks we queried, to their raptures over its charms, wherein lies its loveliness? Oh, it is so lively; you can go to Newport or Wickford or Narragansett Pier, or over to the Fort, or down to the Dumplings or – oh, there's no use talking, Jamestown is perfectly delightful. It would appear from the varied testimony that Jamestown is desirable chiefly for the ease with which one can get out of it; but I suspect that a prime cause of its popularity is its cheapness. There is the great gray Thorndike, with the varied view across the Bay, and the beautiful Bay View, most

Swimming on the Town Beach with Shoreby Hill pier to right.

admirably appointed, and but $2.50 a day, as contrasted with Narragansett Pier's $4 and $5. For natural advantages it has not one-half Conanicut Park's number, or the qualities one actually looks for in a place of summer rest. For all that it is constantly growing; its cottages are multiplying and it has had practically three new hotels in a little more than a year. With the half dozen others, the many boarding places and rooms in cottages, the season here is unusually early and busy. The Thorndike is about to begin a series of afternoon concerts by a string band, hops are in progress, attended with fervor and devotion; bathing is the chief event in the day, in spite of a pebbly and shelly beach.

It is refreshing to see such activity, though it be somewhat confusing to an alien not yet naturalized. The sojourners are not dozing from 3 to 6 p.m. as a general thing, but are walking, driving, rowing, sailing and attending tennis and ball games with the utmost abandon. The excursions on foot are by the

JHS P2017.017.001

The Cliff Walk along the East Passage south of the village.

shore road, north and south, as far as one may list; far northward he may go and go and know no ending, along the pebble beach, whose pebbles, alas! are all angles instead of curves, or over the sloping hill. Southward, there is a "cliff walk" along the sea, beginning modestly enough and gradually rising till the way terminates at the rolling hills and gray crags that drop in the southern sea, where are Conanicut's only fine breakers, and where quaint little Fort Dumpling, like an outcropping of the granite itself, crowns the gray crags, unchristened all these years by the fiery baptism of shot and shell.

From north to south the whole length of the island the main road runs straight as a die, swerving not even for the salt sound that penetrates far inland and broadens into a marshy pond. Beyond it the gray road turns steeply upward over a hill on whose summit the ancient windmill of the island stands with Maltese cross of its gigantic arms sharply outlined against the pale sky. Off to the right is the quaint and interesting old Weeden place, enshrined among trees; then the old Quaker meeting house, where the devotees were wont of yore to solemnly "wait before the Lord" in stately silence, and further north still is the oldest house on the island. On goes the broad highway, bordered by blackberries fiercely thorn-guarded, and the waxen blooms of the clethra, sweetest of all August wild flowers, while down in the marshy brooks behind the wild hedges stands in stately ranks the royal cardinal flower of the Indians. And at last a branch road turns eastward to Conanicut Park, and the traveler is stayed.

At the cross roads near Jamestown, where high road meets ferry way, a southwest avenue leads down to the sandy bar that is the frail connection between east and west Conanicut. Only at supremely high tides is this frail passway flooded, and the walk or drive to western shore is an extremely interesting one, from Beaver Head on the north – though the natives call it Fox Hill – to the lighthouse of Beaver Tail on the wild southern shore, where even yet the lingering spar of the recent wreck grasp imploringly upward out of the water. The cross at the roads is marked by a graveyard on one hand, where on one ancient stone is with difficulty

JHS P2021.306.001

Central Baptist Church about 1900.

JHS P1980.186

The *Jamestown* approaching West Ferry with the hay stacks of Fox Hill Farm in the distance.

deciphered under the veiling moss the name Pauline, and the date 1745; on the other hand, the religion and morals of the Island are represented by an Episcopal Church and one of those white-faced, green-eyed Baptist meeting houses, whose belfries are capped with suggestive spikes.

A mile or so across the Island, from east ferry to west ferry, runs another highway, from Jamestown down to the dock, where a smaller ferry-boat, the *Jamestown*, waits to convey excursionists to Narragansett and back again. By Narragansett, I do not mean the Pier, often erroneously so called, but a wee, gray and ancient village directly opposite Jamestown on the western mainland.

There is no prettier diversion of a summer afternoon than to make a ferry trip east or west among our harbor waters and the many anchored vessels. Westward through Dutch Island harbor and past the peaceful island, where the Sergeant's home stands high among the upland trees and the grassy fortifications, and the southern point is tipped by the light-house of the white light. And off the mainland the break-ers are distantly seen leaping about Bonnet Head, where the *Rhode Island* came to wreck, though the harbor waters lift the little ferry boat with only a gentle swell.

Eastward the big *Conanicut*, plying between Newport and the island, glides between forts and islands and lighthouses galore, and the small boats of the training ship, with her jolly young uniformed lads, or perhaps the white-clad crew of the big Norseman, their vessel's name blazoned on their navy caps, pull lustily across the ferry's pathway.

Jamestown is not lacking for diversions, and though in her quiet waters there is not the delightful acquaintance of the surf to make, there is an equivalent in an opportunity for fancy swimming and safe rowing, of which the young folk are not slow to avail themselves. The bathing beach, though small in extent is a safe and pleasant one, and even a despon-dent on suicide bent would have difficulty in making way with himself by drowning, so many are the skiffs and catboats hovering always about.

All things considered, it is little wonder that Jamestown is a favorite among the young folks, though it is not Provi-dence people, but Southerners and Westerners, notably from St. Louis, who hie here, and the place is already full to over-flowing.

Everybody looks busy and happy, and nobody looks bored, and say what one may, Jamestown is the liveliest, the noisiest, and the most hilarious summer city on the Rhode Island coast.

A COMMUNITY MADE PROSPEROUS IN SPITE OF ITSELF: 1902

by An Old Resident

Fifty or even forty years ago, one who regarded Conanicut Island as other than a fairly promising agricultural district with natural advantages as such, would have been looked upon as the veriest dreamer. Connected with Newport on the east and the Narragansett country on the west by rude sloop ferries, it had comparatively little intercourse with the remainder of the world. The island was not progressive, socially or politically, and was regarded by its own people, to the manor born, as a desirable place only to till the soil, disposing of its surplus products to its neighbors.

It was in reality a charming agricultural district, as such capable of being rendered, with proper cultivation, the garden

JHS P1998.112

Cattle grazing at Hull Cove Farm on Beavertail in the early 20th century.

of Rhode Island. As a community it was almost totally void of ambition, and when the opportunity was offered of becoming a place of resort for health and pleasure, to increase the value of its broad acres many fold, they thrust it from them at every point. The Carrs, the Caswells, the Watsons, and others had for generations dwelt there contentedly as simple agriculturists, and they were content to do so for generations to come. They found a satisfactory market in Newport and elsewhere for their potatoes, corn, butter, eggs, and other products of their farms, and their aspirations rose no higher.

It was not until after the war of the Rebellion that this condition of things was broken in upon, and then only, for a long time, by a single individual, Mr. A. Crawford Greene, a master printer of Providence. Attracted to the beautiful prospect which the section opposite Newport afforded, together with its pure air

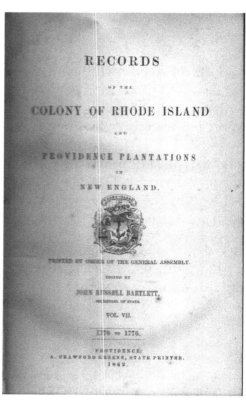

A. Crawford Greene, Jamestown's first summer resident, was the State Printer responsible for printing Rhode Island state records in the Civil War era.

and other rural advantages as a summer resort, he construct-ed a small cottage on the rising ground south of the only road crossing the island in that vicinity and, for a number of years, he brought his family to reside there summers, attending to his business during the week in Providence and spending his Sundays in his Conanicut home.

For ten years, more or less, this state of things continued, and if it occurred to any Jamestowner to enlarge upon it he kept it pretty much to himself, lest he should become among his neighbors an object of ridicule as an idle dreamer. Mean-while the island was attracting attention from a few outsiders, non-residents, regarding it as a desirable place on which to spend the summer months, and the resident farmers received and accepted applications for summer board, and had all they could accommodate.

About this time there was a boom that for a time gave promise, somewhat, of a future that through another chan-nel, became a reality. An enterprising citizen of Newport, with an unusual degree of foresight for this region, albeit he was not to the manor born, saw in his mind what he regarded as great possibilities for the hamlet across the river, in which there figured largely a steam ferry to replace the clumsy and uncomfortable sailing craft then attempting to do duty as such, and he resolved to become a promoter.

His observation of the sturdy population of the Island had taught him that there was little if any hope in that direction. He therefore turned his attention to wealthy men in Provi-dence, resulting in his being authorized to purchase, at a fair valuation, all the farms in the center of the island, or rather to secure option thereon. This he succeeded in doing, except

JHS P1984.203

William H. Knowles, the man "from up the bay."

in one instance, where the owner of a large tract in the very center of the proposed purchase declined to sell. This swamped the plans of the syndicate, whose aim was to develop the place after the manner in which this has since come about, though perhaps differently in some particulars.

About this time there appeared on the scene another promoter, one who was destined to figure prominently in the development of the island as a watering place. Howbeit his primary objective was to promote his own interests, which was natural and legitimate. He was an immigrant from up the bay, with a fair supply of cash and quite a full supply of brains. The antiquated sloop ferry between Jamestown and Newport was for sale, and he bought it. It had not for a considerable time been paying satisfactory dividends, and he resolved the first thing to make an improvement in that particular. The ferry had been run largely for the benefit of the islanders and was regarded as a sort of family or neighborhood arrangement. This he determined to change and did so. The franchise went with the proprietor-

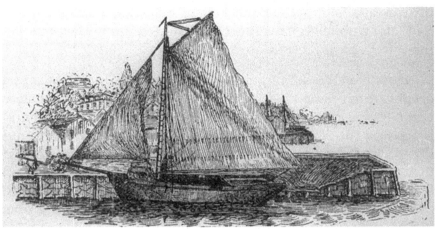

JHS P1971.051

The sailing ferryboat that ran between Ferry Wharf Newport and Jamestown. The plate of the wharf was cut down to accommodate passengers and freight to the rising and falling of the tide.

ship of the ferry, and he had the staff in his own hands. It was evident that there was no way of getting on or off the island except to swim, use a private boat, or accept his terms. These were not always acceptable, in several particulars, and the

JHS P1971.050

The new East Ferry wharf with the ferryboat *Jamestown*, Jamestown's first steam ferry.

disgruntled islanders began to broach and discuss privately, and later publicly, plans for relief. This eventuated in a movement for a steam ferry.

Here was the turning point in the island's fortunes, and a great future opened before its people, though they were slow to recognize and promote it. Steamer *Jamestown* was built and placed on the ferry, the town being a large stockholder, and the sloop ferry boats, finding their occupation gone, furled their sails and prepared to go out of commission. The steam ferry was run for years with dividends scarcely sufficient to pay expenses. One year in particular- the culminating one, by the way, in its fortunes – the deficit was $1,400, and the "I-told-you-so's" appeared to be on top, some even going so far as to propose abandoning the charter and going back to wind as a motive power. But, as was said before, this was the culminating year of the steam ferry's shortcomings, and after that the scale went up more and more each year.

Meanwhile better facilities for travel brought more summer boarders, and slowly and carefully the islanders, or one of them, and this the same individual whose sloop ferry had been knocked out, built a hotel, the first on the island, and the Bay View House, under the management of the late Captain Stephen C. Gardner. To make a long story short, the hotel was a success, and according to his policy, as aforesaid, the owner raised the rent to an unbearable figure. This led to the building of the Gardner House, the success of these two led to the building of others and Jamestown outvied anything in this direction in the way of hotels except Narragansett Pier and Watch Hill.

JHS P1979.016

The original Bay View House, built in 1872 by William H. Knowles. The Ellery House on the corner was later replaced by the Bay View Tower.

In all of this the landed proprietors of the island had been faithless and unbelieving, they had not gone forward of their own volition, but had been urged on by outside pressure till they got a-going and could not stop as the saying is. But as a matter of course the introduction of the cottages followed in the wake of the hotels, and in some instances preceded them, and now, from one little cottage, already referred to, there have come scores, of more or less elegance and magnitude.

One of the earliest cottages built was that of the late George Howland.[1] He was the owner of a tract of land and a substantial farmhouse near the ferry, the house needing some repairs and he resolved that, instead of laying out the two or three thousand dollars necessary to that end, he would build a new house entirely. He accordingly put up a cottage that, before he had it completed and furnished, cost in the neigh-

---

[1] John Howland is the name of the person referred to.

borhood of $25,000. He even had the house piped throughout for gas, though there were not half-a-dozen other cottages on the island, and the prospect for many more was not at the time promising.

Mr. Howland at once became the town's talk. His neighbors said he had got himself into a fix that he would never safely get out of. And it did look so for a while, as there were mortgages and financial difficulties crowding upon the man of three score and ten, or thereabouts, that looked threatening. But whether or not he had seen the light ahead, it came. He held on, and died a comparatively wealthy man.

Jamestown has not reached the summit of its prosperity. There are other lands and building sites not yet developed, north, south, and west of the present settlement, and it will not be many years ere the hotel and cottage colony in the middle of the island will be closely united to that of Conanicut Park.

It is a fact worthy of reiteration that no improvement of any magnitude has ever been made in Jamestown but has been met with vigorous and persistent opposition. When the ferryboat *Conanicut* first made her appearance it was said of her that she was too much boat for the business and would never pay her way, and the *Beaver Tail* was looked at askance for a while. Jamestown will go down in history as a community made rich and prosperous in spite of itself.

A TRIP AROUND JAMESTOWN: 1928

by Walter Leon Watson

Last August I was called to New York. It was during one of those hot spells and New York was torrid. The sidewalks seemed to be melting, and the buildings seemed like furnaces, radiating heat in all directions. The air was lifeless, and all humanity was just wilted. I was heartily thankful when my business was over, and I could take the boat to Fall River.

The next morning, on the train to Newport, I shared the seat with a distinguished looking gentleman, evidently a military man. A general conversation was soon started, but as we drew towards the shore where a view of the bay could be seen, he exclaimed. "Isn't that a beautiful picture." After a minute or two he continued, "I am a commander in the Navy. Have been stationed in Manila for the past year. Have just been assigned shore duty with a three-month leave and took the first boat going east and am not going to stop until I get to Jamestown. I have probably been in every large port or harbor in the world and, to my mind, Narragansett Bay is the most beautiful of them all, and Jamestown is the very heart of the bay." At Newport we separated for he took the first ferry to Jamestown, I a later one.

I immediately went to the upper deck of the beautiful new ferryboat the *Governor Carr*. The New York Yacht Club evidently were on their annual cruise for the inner harbor was full of yachts of all descriptions. As we rounded the break-water, passing into the outer harbor, all sorts of war vessels – cruisers, torpedo boats, and torpedo boat destroyers – were in full view, lying at their moorings and extending up the bay for a mile or more. As we rounded Rose Island the peaceful waters of the bay were bathed in the golden glow of the setting sun. Thirty miles to the north was Providence, and to the south through the East Passage could be seen the undulating water of the ocean. As I stood there, deeply impressed by the beauty of the scene, I said to myself. "Commander, you are right. Jamestown is the heart of Narragansett Bay."

People have been coming to Jamestown, year after year, for 20 and 30 years. Why? Because they have found an ideal place for their summer vacation. All the elements that go to

JHS A2008.700.061

The *Governor Carr* in Jamestown.

make summer the most delightful time of the year are there. The climate is ideal.. It is delightful in June, wonderful in July, gorgeous in August, mellow in September, and revivifying in October.

No breeze passes over the island that has not been cooled and refreshed by either waters of the bay or of the ocean. Every afternoon the prevailing southwest breeze springs up from off the ocean and dies down with the setting sun, leaving the island fresh and peaceful for a refreshing night's sleep. A noted nerve specialist has stated that a night's sleep on Jamestown does more good to jagged nerves than all the medicine he can prescribe.

The greatest asset of Jamestown is that it is on an island. Except for those crossing from ferry to ferry, none come to the island unless they want to be there, and there only. There is no interminable line of tourists with smoking motors, squeaking brakes, and honking horns. The roads of the island can be driven in safety, and the scenery enjoyed.

There is hardly a place on the whole island where there is not a beautiful view, and always different. The east bay is the scene of activity; it is used by all the vessels for Newport, Fall River, and Providence and is the popular place for yachting and boat races. Driving around the north end of the island the west bay comes in view and is quiet and peaceful. To the west is quaint old Wickford nestling among the trees. Stretching to the south is the wooded shoreline of Narragansett, serving as a beautiful green frame for the peaceful blue waters of the bay, dyed a still deeper blue by the reflection of the Venetian blue sky overhead. The west bay is quiet and peaceful. A stray fishing boat may come dreamily up with the tide or the

JHS P1979.006

" 'The First Gun,' The Yacht Club, Jamestown, R.I." From an oil painting by Catharine Morris Wright.

boats at Saunderstown may be having a race, but somehow these only seem to emphasize the peacefulness of the whole scene.

But let us go to the south end of the island through some beautiful woods and then up hill and down dale – the island is by no means flat and uninteresting. As we approach the southern end and the island draws to a point, the shores are high and rocky, and the roar of the mighty ocean greets our ears. What a contrast! Here is action, life, the breeze tastes salty from the ocean, the mighty waves are dashing on the rocks, everything speaks of life. How you long for a good pole and reel to catch that eight-pound black fish that is just off the rocks. What other place is there where in a drive of a few minutes, you can transport yourself from the dreamy waters of an inland bay to the mighty ocean with its endless succession of waves dashing in majestic beauty on the high

JHS A2008.165.027

The Dumplings.

rocky shore? But such is Jamestown, the Heart of Narragan-sett Bay.

The village proper comprises the territory lying between the east and west ferries. Here are stores, garages, boarding-houses, and hotels. To the south, at the Dumplings, so called because the surface of the land is made up of many little hills, are the summer homes of the people from afar off, who come here year after year to enjoy an ideal summer. There is much land here still for those who have not as yet found the summer home of their heart's desire.

A few minutes drive to the north of the village and you are in a farming community. Sheep and cows are grazing in the pasture. Corn and grain are waving in the breeze, vegetable gardens are at either hand, assuring you of a fresh supply of all farm produce. Some of the farmers ship their produce –

JHS A2006.402.001

The planned Conanicut Club. The plans never came to fruition.

particularly eggs, poultry, and turkeys – to their customers after they have returned to their city homes.

Some of the summer residents have preferred the quieter end of the island, so as you drive along the shore road, you see more summer homes interspersed among the farmland. But as you approach the north end of the island you come to a little community of summer folks at Conanicut Park. For nearly a mile to the west, stretching to the shores of the West Passage and also to the south for a mile or more is a vast area of uncultivated land that has recently been acquired by the Conanicut Club. Plans have all been drawn and work started for a wonderful club development, including two 18-hole golf courses, club house, bathing pavilion, tennis courts, and bridle paths.

Yes, Jamestown is the ideal summer playground.

Do you wish to play golf? There are two courses at your command. The Country Club course is just outside the village, within walking distance, while the Audley Clarke course is on the road to Beavertail and its 18 holes extends from ocean to ocean, one of the most scenic courses in the country.

And one of your first acts will be to join the Conanicut Club with its proposed two 18-hole courses.

Do you wish to ride horse back? There are miles of dirt roads such as a horse dearly loves, extending up hill and down dale, through the woods and into the open.

Do you wish surf bathing or do you prefer the quieter waters of the bay? Both are at your disposal. At the beach at Mackerel Cove, the Town has erected a large modern bath house, and the waters of the ocean break on the sandy beach in a succession of "breakers." The long slope of the beach reduces the undertow so that bathing here is perfectly safe. Then there is the quiet water of the bay where swimming can be enjoyed to the utmost.

Do you wish to fish? Tautog abound off Beavertail. Nothing will delight Captain Manders, at the lighthouse, more than to direct you to Bold Caesar, Old Slippery, Yellow Dirt, Flint, or Bass Rock and tell you just how far and in what direction to cast. You can catch black fish weighing from two to ten pounds, sea bass weighing up to 75 pounds – if you know

JHS P2012.029.019

Fishing pier at Beavertail.

JHS P2004M.406

Hydroplane moored in Potters Cove.

how. For trolling or spearing, a power boat will give a day's outing off Block Island trolling for tuna or spearing sword-fish.

Do you wish hotel life? The Bay Voyage, Gardner Inn, Maplewood, Thorndyke, Bay View, and Point View will all be glad to extend a cordial invitation to avail yourselves of the facilities of their modern hotels, only make your reservations early.

Do you wish dancing? Membership in the Casino is all that is necessary, the club house and orchestra are for your pleasure.

Will you bring your own car? There is Brook's Garage, Richardson's Garage, Central Garage, and Jamestown Garage with their expert service to relieve you of all worry.

And now let us take a little drive around the island. Dinner is over and the long summer evening has begun. We start from the ferry and go north on the shore road. Shoreby Hill with its beautiful colonial houses is on our left with the Casino just off the road. Up a slight grade, we pass the Bay Voyage and Maplewood Hotels and the outlying cottages of the village. On the left is the Country Club golf links. After a slight turn and down the hill, there on the right in Potters Cove are 20 or 30 hydroplanes of all sizes riding at anchor after the day's activities. The big mother ship is at anchor farther out in the bay.

Passing a few cottages at the foot of the hill we approach the farms, cows and sheep are grazing in the pasture, hens and chickens are going to rest, and the farmer is busy preparing the next day's work. And now we come to a beautiful patch of woods. In the olden days every farm had its wood lot and many of these are still preserved. All the way the waters of the bay are in full view. Gould Island with its fringe of fir trees is soon passed. It is but a mile long, and as we

JHS P2017.103.011

Driving up Beavertail Road with Mackerel Cove beyond the fields.

approach the "Park" the south of Prudence appears. Here we turn a sharp left and up a hill and stop for a minute to enjoy the beauty of the scene. The peaceful waters of the bay stretch before our gaze, a faint breeze ruffles the surface of the water and the little ripples are dancing merrily hither and yon bathing themselves in the golden red rays of the setting sun.

But on we go through Love Lane. For nearly a mile we go through the woods. All is still save for the evening song of the song sparrow. The air smells woodsy, and the shadows grow deeper and deeper. Out of the woods and up a hill and we are on the crown of the island. At the head of Carr's Lane we alight and climb the hill on our right to the highest point on the island. The sun has disappeared, but the glorious afterglow has turned the sky a wonderful red and gold which is reflected in the water. Plum Beach Light is winking at us, and the lights at Saunderstown are beginning to appear.

But it is the full of the moon, and we have an objective, so hurry on past the old windmill and the Quaker Meeting House, past Ferry Road, over the beach where we were in bathing, up the hill past the farms and the Clarke Golf Course to Beaver Tail. Right down to the point we go. The afterglow of the setting sun has gone, and in the deep shadows of early evening we see Whale Rock light, the lights of Narragansett Pier, Point Judith light, Block Island light, Brenton's Reef light, Castle Hill light, and the faint reflection of the lights of Newport. The waves of the ocean at our feet seem to be growing lazy, the swish and swirl of the breaking waves takes a deeper and softer tone. After a while comes the glory of the rising moon, and the golden-tinted silver rays stretch across the undulating surface of the ocean in an ever widening path.

JHS P2019.200.197

Moonlight on Narragansett Bay.

Higher and higher it rises, brighter and brighter grows the scene until it is almost day again, but a softened day, a day of dreams and introspection.

We hesitate long before we start the motor and travel along back past the farms and around Dumpling Road and past the entrance of the bay. Here the harbor is in full view. It is like fairy land. The war vessels are twinkling with hundreds of lights, the search-lights are waving across the heavens, launches hurrying hither and yon in the moonlight, the seductive strains of a waltz come floating across the water from one war vessel where a dance is being held. Aladdin with his magic lamp could produce no more entrancing scene than this.

JHS P1997.072

The U.S. Fleet off Jamestown.

"Shall we stay here a while and enjoy the picture or go to the Casino?"

"As you please, my dear, either would be wonderful."

Such is Jamestown, the Heart of Narragansett Bay.

Preserving Our History and Our Environment

INTRODUCTION

Farming was the primary occupation in Jamestown until the late 19ᵗʰ century. The potential of the island as a resort was first recognized by men from Newport and Providence who developed Conanicut Park at the North End as a summer retreat for Providence families beginning in 1872. The following year, the steam ferry between Jamestown village and Newport began.

The transition from agricultural backwater to summer resort was underway.

Farms were subdivided so summer visitors and those who arrived to make their visits attractive would have places to live. Hotels were built, changing the waterfront and the village. New and expanded services, from restaurants to electricity, followed.

Not all Jamestowners were convinced that this "progress" was positive. Much of both historic and environmental importance was being lost.

Summer visitors, perhaps because it was the history and atmosphere of the island that caused them to summer here, were the first to take action. The derelict windmill was an attractive part of the vanishing agricultural world. They formed the Jamestown Windmill Association to keep the mill from falling down.

Other preservation efforts followed, usually spearheaded by a small cadre of dedicated residents. These essays discuss only a few. The total land preserved by historical and environmental organizations is approximately 29 percent of the island.

JAMESTOWN'S FIRST PRESERVATION EFFORT: THE JAMESTOWN WINDMILL

The first organization in Jamestown formed to preserve the history of Conanicut Island was the Jamestown Windmill Association, founded in 1904. The organization's sole purpose was to purchase and preserve the Jamestown windmill.

Background

The current Jamestown gristmill was built in 1787, shortly after the American Revolution. It was used primarily to grind dried kernels of white flint corn, also called Indian corn, into cornmeal for human consumption and into silage for animals.

Over 110 years, 14 millers successively operated the mill. Thomas and Jesse Tefft, the last millers, closed the mill in 1896, driven out of business by the large rolling

Courtesy of Rosemary Enright

The Jamestown windmill in 1902, shortly before the purchase.

103

mills of the Midwest. Jesse occasionally ground cornmeal in 1897 before closing the mill for good.

Saving the Mill

For seven years, the mill stood neglected. Equipment was removed or destroyed. Weather took its toll. In 1904, the mill's pitiful condition led residents and summer visitors to form the Jamestown Windmill Association. They circulated a petition to raise money to buy the derelict building.

Sixty Jamestowners contributed over $700 toward the purchase and repair of the mill. The contributions varied in size from $50 from each of three members of the summer community to 50¢ from Annie Barber, a native Rhode Islander who worked as a companion to a member of the Carr family.

On October 19, 1904, Thomas Tefft sold "the mill and land enough to drive around it" –

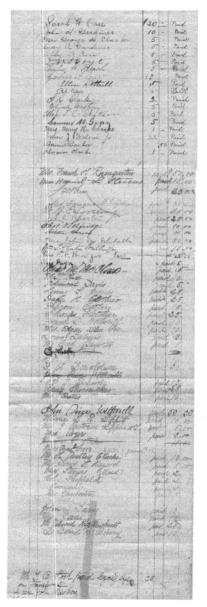

List of pledges to save the Jamestown windmill.

about 3,600 square feet – to Mary Rosengarten, the representative of the Association, for $300. Because of this early intervention, the Jamestown mill is the only one of its kind in Rhode Island to remain on its original site.

For eight years, the Windmill Association kept the mill from deteriorating further. Thomas D. Wright, a Jamestown builder and carpenter, was hired to make repairs, and a caretaker was appointed. However, the unincorporated group was loosely structured, and the stewardship of the mill rested heavily on Mrs. Rosengarten's shoulders.

Jamestown Historical Society

In the summer of 1912, Elizabeth Carr Locke, a California-based descendant of Caleb Carr who often returned to Jamestown for the summer, conceived the idea of forming a historical society in Jamestown. She had 200 posters printed and distributed around the island asking anybody interested in forming such a society to meet at Town Hall on August 19.

On the appointed day, 26 men and women gathered in Town Hall. The minutes of that meeting record the actions taken:

> *A motion was made and seconded to organize the Society and name it later. Carried.*
>
> *Voted to nominate officers and they were elected as follows:*

JHS A2021.504.033 pic 17

Lena Clarke, first president of the historical society.

President – Miss Lena Clarke
Vice President – Mrs. Chas. E. Weeden
Secretary – S[arah] W. Carr
Treasurer – Mrs. John F. Weeden

Voted that the President appoint a Committee to draw up a Constitution and by-laws: Mrs. Locke, Dr. [W. Lincoln] Bates, T. Carr Watson, Giles Carr Gardiner, S.W. Carr were appointed for that purpose.

Voted that membership fee is $1.00.

Voted that yearly dues be $1.00.

Voted, after some discussion that the Society be called the Jamestown Historical Society. [The alternative proposed was the Conanicut Historical Society.]

. . .

It was voted that a committee of three be appointed to consult Mrs. Rosengarten in relation to combining the Windmill Association with the Historical Society.

The leaders of the new organization moved quickly. On August 26, at the second meeting of the Society, a constitution and bylaws were presented and accepted. On September 10, 1912, the state issued a charter to Lena H. Clarke, Elizabeth Carr Locke, Sarah W. Carr, Josephine A. Weeden, and Herbert Head that incorporated the Jamestown Historical Society with "the purpose of preserving old land marks and collection of historical relics."

On October 7, following a vote by the members of the Jamestown Windmill Association many of whom were also members of the new historical society, Mrs. Rosengarten

JHS P1984.132

John F Carr's daughter, Louise, donated the lot south of the windmill.

transferred ownership of the Jamestown windmill to the Jamestown Historical Society. As a condition of the transfer the society would preserve the windmill "at all times hereafter forever for the benefit of the public of said Town [Jamestown] and as and for a landmark of historic interest."

The deed included the 3,600 square feet around the mill itself and a half-acre of land to the south of the mill, which had been donated to the Windmill Association by the Carr family. The Carr gift provided direct access to North Main Road.

Maintaining the Preserved Mill

When the historical society acquired the Jamestown windmill from the Jamestown Windmill Association, the windmill was in need of work that the new organization could not afford. Vandals had removed everything movable from inside the mill. The block and tackle for moving the stone had disappeared. The hopper and shoe that fed the grain into the grinding stones were gone. Missing parts were replaced slowly by purchase, gift, or construction. Pillars identifying the entrance to the property and a stone wall on the west side as a fire break were erected in 1921.

Major Conservation Efforts

Approximately every 20 years, major conservation efforts have been required in order to keep the mill in good shape.

1933-1934. By 1933, it became obvious that a major restoration would be necessary even if the mill were never used again to grind grain. At the July meeting, the Society's president Peyton Hazard reported that the windmill "should be almost rebuilt." Over the following year, rotted sills were replaced, footings were leveled, and a firm concrete foundation was poured. The mill was opened for visitors again in July 1934 and survived the Hurricane of 1938 in relatively good shape.

1968-1970. The windmill suffered greatly in the 1950s. A 1953 winter storm blew off two arms and some of the bonnet. The windmill lost another arm in Hurricane Carol in 1954. The arms were restored in time for the 1957 tercentenary of the purchase of the island, but funding did not cover repairs needed to the bonnet, and the arms were fixed facing southwest. A major renovation began in June 1968. Some furniture and equipment were salvaged from a soon-to-be-demolished mill at Davisville. A new

JHS P1977.026

Bonnet track and the gears to turn the bonnet restored during 1968 renovation.

wind-shaft was hand-cut from yellow pine stock. The bonnet was reframed and seated on the metal track that allowed it to be turned to the wind. The stones were sharpened, or "dressed."

1981. The 1981 work focused on structural weaknesses of the mill building. Beams, especially floor joists, were replaced. New doors were built. The renova-

JHS P2019.111.005

Structural issues identified in preparation for the 1981 work.

tion was combined with an archaeological dig in an attempt to answer questions about the previous use of the land and the existence of an earlier mill on the same spot.

2000-2001. The renovation begun in 2000 saw the windmill completely stripped of its shingles and the bonnet removed for reshingling.

A new wind shaft was formed and positioned in the bonnet. New sails were built. It was a two-year project.

2020-2021. Wood for a new wind shaft was aging in the field next to the mill in 2020 when the COVID pandemic forced the mill to be closed to visitors. Work continued on the repairs, though at a slower pace. The new wind shaft and sails were finally installed in time for a successful opening in June 2022.

All of these major renovations required grants and gifts from outside sources, including the Champlin Foundations, the Rhode Island Foundation, and other local foundations and organizations.

On-going Maintenance

Concern about day-to-day upkeep of the windmill was relieved by an endowment established in 1987 by two sisters, Nan Thompson and Margaret Evans. The annual income from the fund and from a smaller endowment at the Rhode Island Foundation is sufficient to pay for normal maintenance of the mill and grounds, if nothing exceptional occurs.

In 2010, the Society's received a Conservation

JHS A2014.025.006

The 2000-2001 renovation (top to bottom). Reshingling the bonnet. Positioning the newly formed wind shaft. Replacing the bonnet.

Assessment Program (CAP) grant to identify the outstanding needs and priorities for the preservation of its collections

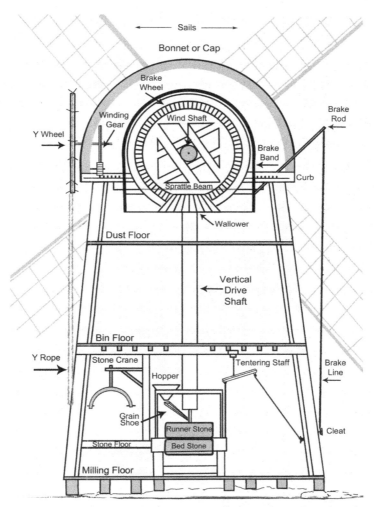

Diagram of the Jamestown windmill developed under the RICH grant to improve signage in the mill.

and buildings. The assessors recommended several improvements to the windmill, including exterior signage for those unable to climb to the top of the mill and improved displays and safety features inside.

A Rhode Island Council for Humanities (RICH) grant helped pay for the exterior signage installed in 2012. A second RICH grant was awarded to improve the interior signage and displays. Incremental improvements continue to be made to enhance visitors' enjoyment and understanding of the site.

The Jamestown windmill was placed on the National Register of Historic Places in 1973. It has been open on summer weekends – except when repairs prevented it – since the late 1950s. Both fulfill the conditions of the original deed that it be a "benefit of the public" of Jamestown and "landmark of historic interest."

SAVING THE SALT MARSH

The Great Creek and the salt marshes on either side of it separate the north end of Conanicut Island from the village. In the early days, they were a true barrier, forcing north-enders to detour across the neck on the east side where the bridge buildings are now. Later some saw the barrier as a possible water route between Newport and the west; proposals for a canal through the marsh first surfaced in 1824. During the next 100 years, other proposals included marinas and hotels.

At a meeting of the Jamestown Garden Club in August 1950, Helen Marshall Eliason, chair of the club's Committee on Public Relations, put forward an entirely different kind of

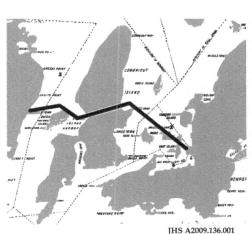

JHS A2009.136.001

The proposed ferry route through a canal in Round Swamp.

proposal. She suggested that, as the club's project for the coming year, it purchase a tract of salt marshland to be given to the town and held in perpetuity as a wildlife preserve. The land she had in mind was the "Conanicut Salt Meadow" north of the Great Creek on the eastern side of North Road.

JHS 1986.015.008

This watercolor of the salt marsh was painted by Mary Marshall whose daughter Helen proposed the project to protect the marsh.

In her presentation, Eliason praised the natural beauty of the area and pointed out the advantages of preserving and restoring the plants – particularly pink mallow and sea lavender marsh heather – that had once flourished there.

Environmentalism was not yet the movement that it is today, but the club members took up the project with enthusiasm. Under Eliason's leadership, they undertook the necessary research and fundraising to make the preservation a reality.

They invited Russell Albright, a state soil conservationist, to evaluate the area. He responded positively. The conservation of the marsh would be "a very valuable addition to marsh plant and wild life." His opinion was endorsed by Ronald C. Clement, the director of the Rhode Island Audubon Society, who also provided a detailed report on the plants, birds, and marine life that lived in the marsh.

The Town Council agreed that the town would accept the gift of the wild life preserve.

The price of the 27½ acres of marsh just north of the Jamestown Golf Course, then the Conanicut Country Club, was $750. The Jamestown Garden Club allocated $400 toward the purchase. Thayer Keeler and Dorothy Lyon began the drive to collect the rest. An early contribution from the recently formed Quononoquot Garden Club gave both financial and moral support. Townspeople pitched in generously. By mid-January 1951, $1,337 had been collected. After the purchase of the property, the $562.28 remaining was put aside for the purchase of surrounding land as it became available.

The only hurdle left was the formal acceptance of the gift by the town. The voters accepted the transfer at the Financial Town Meeting on May 7, 1952. The conditions of conveyance are spelled out in the deed: "the grantees and their successors shall use the premises for recreation purposes as a wildlife

Thayer Keeler (left) and Dorothy Lyon (right) led the drive to raise funds to purchase the salt mash.

JHS P2011.030.004

JHS P1993.068

115

preserve and upon use of the premises for any other purpose, title to the premises shall forthwith revert to the grantors or their successors."

The garden club followed up its successful drive to save the salt marsh with a statement of purpose that incorporated its aims. "This is not nature tailored to a park but a wild area to be kept in its own pattern with no intrusion of foreign material. We hope that the native American scene will be preserved through these small windows opening on a past which is rapidly disappearing and will remind Americans of the undisturbed beauty of their land as their forefathers knew it."

The work of the Jamestown Garden Club did not go unnoticed. In 1953, the club received both the gold medal from the Federation of Garden Clubs of Rhode Island and the National Council of State Garden Clubs Civic Award for its marsh preservation project.

PRESERVING THE 1776 CONANICUT BATTERY

Colonial Period

During the early days of the American Revolution, the fear of attack from the sea drove the defensive activities of Rhode Island rebels. Jamestown originally played a part in their plans.

A sea-borne enemy intent on attacking either Newport or cities farther up the bay had to sail by Conanicut Island either on the east or the west. In the East Passage, the ships would have to pass through the choke point between the Dumplings and what is now Fort Adams under the guns of a well-protected city. In the West Passage, they would be screened by Conanicut from Newport's guns.

Jamestown's Conanicut Battery on Prospect

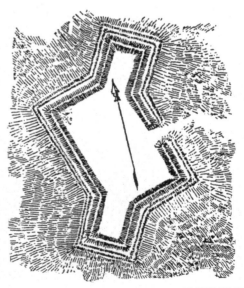

JHS A2019.501.101
A basic map of the Conanicut Battery.

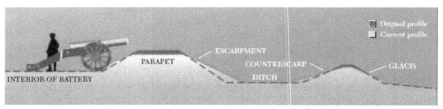

Illustration courtesy of Thomas Paterson

Contour of Conanicut Battery during the British occupation.

Hill at the northern end of Beavertail was built to counter that advantage.

On December 7, 1776, the British did sail up the West Passage as expected. But by that time, the colonists had abandoned Conanicut Island. By order of the General Assembly, livestock had been moved to North Kingstown to prevent the food from falling into British hands. The town government and most of the farmers soon followed.

Lieutenant Frederick Mackenzie, adjutant of the Royal Welch fusiliers, recorded the voyage of the British fleet as it

A2016.601.060

Artillery in place on the battery battlements. During the Revolution, the view of the West Passage would have been unobscured.

passed Conanicut Island: "About two miles from the light house, the Rebels had a battery or redoubt with 4 embrazures toward the channel. But it appeared to be abandoned."

The British-led troops – approximately 6,000 strong – circled Jamestown, landed in Middletown, and entered Newport from the north unopposed. On December 12, the British sent a detachment from their 54th Regiment to Conanicut Island "to take possession of it and protect the inhabitants." A week later, the whole regiment was quartered on the island. The following summer, a detachment of Hessians joined it.

The British occupied Jamestown for almost three years. During this period the only shots known to have been fired at the Conanicut Battery were fired by the British. On July 30, 1778, the *Sagittaire,* a fifty-gun ship from the French fleet attacking British-held Newport, sailed up the West Passage. The guns in Conanicut Battery fired four 24-pound shot at the incoming ship. The *Sagittaire* returned fire. No damage was done on either side. The small detachment manning the battery disabled its guns and quickly withdrew across the East Passage to the safety of Newport.

The campaign to free Newport and Jamestown from British occupation ended with the colonial defeat in the Battle of Rhode Island on August 29, 1778, and British domination of Conanicut Island was reestablished soon after.

At last, on October 25, 1779, the British and Hessian troops evacuated Newport and Jamestown to join the British forces in the southern colonies. For nine months, the fort was abandoned. Then in July 1780 the French under Jean-Baptiste

Donatien de Vimeur, comte de Rochambeau, returned. Some of the French were stationed in Jamestown. They patrolled the island until the British defeat at Yorktown in October 1781.

Twentieth Century

For over a century after the War for Independence, the military showed little interest in Conanicut Island and none whatsoever to the colonial battlements on the West Passage. The area returned to farmland. While nothing was done to preserve the contours of the fortifications, no major changes were introduced. The battlements and Prospect Hill above were kept clear of vegetation by grazing animals and the undulating contours of the battlements continued to be visible despite some erosion.

Illustration by Dave Weyermann

World War I observation posts. Illustration (above) shows ladder leading from manhole-like entry to the observation level. Photograph (below) shows observers in action.

Courtesy of Walter Schroder

The deteriorating fort first came to the attention of the three-year-old Jamestown Historical Society in 1915. Lena Clarke, the Society's president, informed the August meeting that the property was about to be platted. She urged that the society try to preserve the fort as a landmark. Maude Stevens reported at the next meeting that the old fort was to be preserved without society involvement. The following year in preparation for the country's entry into World War I, the federal government built six observation posts on the hill above the old earthworks, taking advantage of the clear view of both the East and West Passages that the pastureland provided.

JHS P2008.023.001

Helen Tefft, Regent of John Eldred Chapter of the Daughters of the American Revolution, cleaning the DAR marker at the Conanicut Battery.

The six observation posts on the crest of Prospect Hill were low lying structures, practically undetectable from a ship. The observers, looking through ground level observation ports, used sighting instruments to take bearings on potential targets and telephoned the data to the gun batteries at forts around the bay.

At the end of the war, once again the military abandoned the battery. This time the Daughters of the American Revolution – the DAR – worked to preserve the land and to ensure that the configuration of the earthenwork battlements were maintained. The organization placed a marker there in 1931 and maintained it until the military once again showed interest in the land as World War II loomed.

The military usefulness of the Conanicut Battery in World War II was minor. Most of the observation tasks that had given the area military value in World War I were transferred to the Harbor Entrance Command Post near the Beavertail lighthouse. Only as the eastern terminus of submarine mines in the West Passage did the battery contribute significantly to the war effort.

The United States Army deeded the 22-acre fort, already

neglected and overgrown, to the town in 1963, noting that repurposing the area as an historic park would preserve a fragile remnant of the country's fight for independence.

Ed Connelly, who led the effort to reclaim the battery.

Ten years later the Conanicut Battery was placed on the National Register of Historic Places, and a revival of the area as a centennial park was proposed. The revival effort was unsuccessful, and for the next 20 years, the park lay neglected.

In 1993, Edwin W. Connelly, a U.S. Army veteran and dedicated history buff, again brought the area to the attention of the Jamestown Historical Society. He wrote in the historical society newsletter "Clearly the old Conanicut Battery on Prospect Hill had a fascinating past, has a deplorable present, and hopefully may have a bright future."

The bright future was almost ten years in coming. In 1997, Connelly organized the Friends of the Conanicut Battery, an independent non-profit organization under the financial umbrella of the historical society, to clean up the park.

Volunteers worked steadily for five years to clear the colonial fortifications and to build trails through the woodlands to reach both the colonial battlements and the World War I observation posts on the hill above them. They raised over $125,000 to fund the effort and to create an endowment that would ensure that the evidence of Jamestown's part in the fight for independence would continue to be maintained.

JHS P2014.114.001

Reenactors representing colonial, English, and French forces participated in the park rededication ceremonies in 2002.

Battery Day 2011

A demonstration of colonial military tactics is enacted at the biennial Battery Day celebration.

The park was rededicated in June 2002. It was a grand affair, with reenactors providing a colorful background for the historical event.

Since that time, the Jamestown Historical Society has worked with the town to improve the trails, re-establish vegetation that would have been common in the Revolutionary War era, and keep the historic portions of the park in good repair. A biennial Battery Day celebration keeps alive community awareness of the importance of this historic site.

Improving Our Town

INTRODUCTION

Government institutions cannot address all the ills of society, although how town government is organized has a big impact on the health of the town. Non-governmental organizations usually work side by side with government to promote and improve the social and political conditions of society on a broad scale. On a local level, they usually have a social aspect and offer opportunities for networking with others with similar interests.

Several types of organizations designed to improve the town have existed in Jamestown over the years.

Some have been dedicated to ensuring that the public is educated on important issues. Among early organizations of this type were three debating societies that met in the 19th and early 20th century. These societies raised awareness by holding formal debates on topics such as slavery, temperance, and woman's place in society. Later Jamestown organizations dedicated to keeping the public informed included the Jamestown Forum.

Service organizations are dedicated to giving direct aid to all or a specific segment of society. The Conanicut Grange is devoted to promoting farming. The Conanicut Council of Royal Arcanum was committed to "giving moral and material aid to its members" and to "teaching morality without religious distinction." Both local chapters met for the first time in 1889. The Jamestown Rotary today raises money to address both local and world-wide issues.

Trade associations support business. Four years after President Calvin Coolidge said "the chief business of the American people is business," Jamestown businessmen organized Jamestown's own Board of Trade to promote Jamestown businesses. The group later became the Chamber of Commerce.

JAMESTOWN BOARD OF TRADE

In May 1929, 21 Jamestowners met at Town Hall to form an organization to "promote the economic, civic, and social welfare of the people of Jamestown and vicinity." The founding members were all Jamestown businessmen, most with businesses at East Ferry or on Narragansett Avenue. Although the group did not exclude summer residents, its primary interest was to improve the business climate in Jamestown, which in large part meant providing better services for those summer visitors.

In the first year, several business interests sought their support. George S. Wilbur came forward to explain the details of the Conanicut Club, an elaborate country club to be

JHS P1986.104

Wyndeswepe, the club house for Audley Clarke's 18-hole golf course on Beavertail.

established at the north end. Audley Clarke, who had built an 18-hole golf course on Beavertail in 1926, came looking for backing for a five-year tax exemption for a new hotel that he planned south of the golf course. Linked to his request was a proposal to move the West Bay terminal of the Jamestown & Newport

Ferry to Orchard Road, an extension of Weeden Lane. The route would shorten the water passage from Saunderstown but would, as many pointed out, make access to the town harder.

The economic downturn of the early 1930s destroyed the idea of any immediate expansion of the resort economy. The Conanicut Club died a quiet death. Clarke's Beaver Tail Country Club struggled on into the 1940s, but without a new hotel. The move of the West Ferry terminal was voted down 376 to 252.

In the meantime, the Board of Trade turned to the much more urgent task of finding work for unemployed residents dislocated by the Great Depression and to other local concerns.

In January 1931, as the depression deepened, the Board of Trade sent letters to 100 summer residents asking that they contract for repairs to their summer homes at once, both to relieve the unemployment and to lessen the congestion later in the spring. The reply was heartening. Over the next years, with state and federal funds, supplemented by funds raised by the Board of Trade and other local organizations, the town weathered the economic storm.

Other concerns also involved the group.

One continuing campaign was for a bank. There were no banks on the island. Summer residents had no immediate access to their funds elsewhere. Local businesses had to keep more cash on hand than was practical or safe. Bankers from Newport were reluctant to establish a Jamestown branch because they feared that business would not be of a type to generate sufficient income and would be practically non-existent during the winter months. A bank was not available in Jamestown until 1958 when Industrial National Bank opened a branch at Narragansett Avenue and Green Lane.

Board of Trade's New Year's greeting to summer residents in 1933.

ON behalf of the townspeople of Jamestown, we wish to express our pleasure at your summer visits to our island, and our hope that we shall see you again.

It never has been our purpose to capitalize on the natural vacation facilities of Jamestown by indiscriminate advertising, preferring that any publicity shall be given by our summer friends, who thereby will be assured of having congenial neighbors during their stay here.

We consider our visitors our guests and sincerely trust you will speak to your friends of the beauties of our island and the delights of spending the summer vacation at Jamestown, "The Heart of Narragansett Bay."

Sincerely yours,
JAMESTOWN BOARD OF TRADE

Jamestown
Rhode Island

JHS A2006.061.001

Working with their local congressman, they successfully arranged for full-time letter carriers beginning in August 1931, contingent on the installation of proper mail receptacles and on the proper numbering of buildings.

With the Westerly Chamber of Commerce, they decried the building of a new road paralleling what is now I95 since it would move traffic inland away from the shore resorts and the ferry to Jamestown.

When a bridge across the Providence River was proposed in 1932, the Board of Trade joined with the Newport Chamber of Commerce in opposing the construction bonds because the bridge would offer a shorter route to Cape Cod, reducing tourism in the two southern towns.

They lobbied strongly for the Jamestown Bridge, even after the State Emergency Public Works Commission had opposed it.

Jamestown's first zoning code was written in the early 1930s and enacted in 1935. The Board of Trade followed the development and, at times, lobbied for provisions.

Through it all the Board of Trade continued to work on advertising the island. At times, the advertising was subtle, as in 1933 when they sent New Year's cards to all summer residents saying "we consider our visitors our guests and sincerely trust you will speak to your friends of the beauties of our island." At others, it was more direct and included distribution of the ferry timetable.

At its annual meeting in 1939, the members of the Board of Trade voted to change the name of the organization to the Jamestown Chamber of Commerce.

"SERVICE ABOVE SELF" — THE JAMESTOWN ROTARY

The Jamestown Rotary Club was born on March 4, 1941.

Over 200 people came to the Jamestown Rotary's Charter Night celebration at the Grange Hall that evening. Clubs from across the area were represented. George R. Ellis, the district governor of District 7950, which encompasses Rhode Island, southeastern Massachusetts, Cape Cod, and the islands of Martha's Vineyard and Nantucket, presented the official charter of the new club to Fred C. Clarke, its first president. A large contingent from the Newport Rotary, which had sponsored the Jamestown club, attended. Their president presented the Jamestown club with a bell, which is still used to call the club's meetings to order, and a gavel.

JHS P2011.031.006

Fred C. Clarke, Sr., first president of the Jamestown Rotary.

JHS 2016.104.002

Jamestown Rotary pennant.

The European war that within the year would become World War II was already affecting Jamestown. Among the first activities sponsored by the new organization was to arrange with the Jamestown 4-H Poultry Club to distribute 100 chickens to help stimulate interest in poultry practices; their project was arranged under the defense nutrition and food production program. Throughout the war, the club members focused on supporting the defense efforts. They conducted house to house canvasses for war bonds, raised money for the Jamestown Red Cross, and provided drivers for the Red Cross ambulance.

In the years after the war, the Jamestown Rotary began a program of college scholarships for Jamestown teens, sponsored international student exchanges, and one year took the eighth graders to a baseball game in Boston. Each November, Rotarians distribute food to less affluent Jamestowners to ensure that Thanksgiving is a feast day for everybody. Local non-profit organizations – from the Jamestown Fire Department to the Jamestown Historical Society – have received gifts to fund special projects. Originally an all-male organization with a women's auxiliary known as "Rotary Anns," females

Courtesy of *The Jamestown Press*

Representative Bruce Long joined John Grant and other Rotarians to serve the May breakfast in 2006.

were admitted to full membership following a Supreme Court decision in 1987.

In 1964, the Jamestown Rotary began a tradition that was to last almost half a century – the Rotary-sponsored May Breakfast. For 48 years, Rotarians in aprons and, sometimes, chef's hats served fruit, eggs, sausages, pancakes, and hash browns, followed by pies and other desserts, at the low-cost, all-you-can eat affair.

In 2013, beset by diminishing attendance and rising costs, the club dropped the May Breakfast in favor of a community picnic. The picnic brought more than 20 non-profit and community service organizations together at the Fort Getty pavilion to publicize their activities.

The Rotary Club also gave Jamestown its town flag. Although Jamestown evidently had a flag during the Revo-

JHS 2012.015.001

Jamestown flag first flown in 1977.

lutionary War period, none was used in the 19th or early 20th century. The Rotary Club designed a flag for the town and presented it to the Town Council. It was flown for the first time at the Town Hall on April 16, 1977.

In the center of the flag is an image of a sheep on a dark green shield. The sheep, which is also on the Town Seal, is a reference to the island's long pastoral tradition. The flag has been changed slightly since then to include the date of incorporation.

All of these activities require money to pay for them, and in 1973 the Rotary Club members began an annual fund-rais-

JHS P2014.004.018

Start of the Around-the-Island bike race, 1994.

ing event that succeeded beyond their wildest expectation – the Jamestown Classic Around-the-Island bike race. Initially the Columbus Day race was a relatively small, local affair. In 1980, it attracted fewer than 60 riders. The numbers rose quickly – 210 cyclists followed the 22-mile route in 1990 and over 500 came in 2015.

While proud of the success of their race sponsorship, the Rotarians were aware of the disruption that the influx of bikers and their teams caused on the island. In 2015, they hired a firm to gauge the level of community support and the economic impact.

As a result of the study, many changes were made for the 2016 race. The race now launches from Fort Getty on the Sunday before Columbus Day, rather than from the Recreation Center on Columbus Day itself. From Fort Getty, the course – slightly shortened from 22 to 19 miles – loops south to Beavertail and then follows Beavertail Road, Southwest Avenue, and North Road to Summit Avenue on the North

Courtesy of *The Jamestown Press*

Leaders in the 2019 Jamestown Classic rounding Beavertail.

End. It returns to Fort Getty by the same route, avoiding the village center.

The fallout of all these changes is that the race is more manageable and less stressful for the people of Jamestown. It is also less profitable than earlier years but still contributes substantially to Rotary charities.

The proceeds from recent races have allowed the club to contribute to a number of local, national, and international causes. Locally, the Rotary has purchased new music chairs for the Jamestown Middle School, sponsored an after-school piano concert, bought specialty clothing for tiny premature and sick infants, and supported the Jamestown Boy Scouts. Outside the immediate area, funds have gone to research for a cure to ALS (Lou Gehrig's Disease), the purchase of wheel-chairs for underprivileged individuals in Nicaragua, the creation of a women's literacy project in Ghana, and assisting in the maintenance of a clean water project in Cambodia. In 2022, the entire proceeds, $8,000, supported the Jamestown Ukrainian Relief Project.

The Jamestown Rotary Club remains a small group of men and women – 22 members in 2022 – who meet weekly in a friendly, collegial atmosphere. Breakfast meetings alter-nate with dinner meetings to accommodate schedules. At most meetings, an invited speaker addresses the group on a current topic of interest. The subjects are diverse. Over the years, topics have included developments in television (1953), conservation at Beavertail State Park (1989), and slavery in Jamestown (2016).

THE JAMESTOWN FORUM

In the aftermath of World War II, the world faced the twin tasks of recovering from the dislocations that had affected everyone's life and of defining the future direction of society. Many new governmental organizations were founded – from the United Nations (October 1945) at the international level to the Jamestown Planning Commission (authorized January 1945, instituted April 1947) at the local level.

Non-governmental organizations were also formed to address the problems ahead, among them the Jamestown Forum, which first entered the public eye in 1947. The aim of the new organization was "to promote the civic betterment, the public improvement, and the general welfare of the Town of Jamestown." The group specifically denied being a political action committee, although throughout its eight-year history it took stands on most problems that confronted the town. In 1952, the Forum's success in gathering facts and making them available to the public inspired a similar group to be formed in Middletown.

Among the first issues the Forum tackled was a bridge from Jamestown to Newport. The Town of Jamestown, in the form of the elected Jamestown Bridge Commission, had built the 1940 Jamestown Bridge. The Town also owned the Jamestown-Newport ferry system. The obvious next step was a bridge to Newport. Jamestowners questioned who would

Courtesy of James C. Buttrick
Commodore Cary W. Magruder.

build it, how it would be paid for, where would it go, and when – questions that weren't answered until the mid-1960s.

The Forum turned its attention to the related problem of travel between the Jamestown Bridge and the ferry wharf at the end of Narragansett Avenue. With the end of World War II gas rationing, traffic on the Jamestown Bridge increased. Cars, trucks, and buses were routed across the two-lane Eldred Avenue and down East Shore Road. The Forum floated a plan to reroute the traffic down North Road and across Narragansett Avenue. The suggestion went nowhere.

The group had more success with its support of Jamestown Bridge Commission transparency. For its first 15 years, the commission issued no reports or minutes. Criticisms of the commission's activities were aired at several Forum meetings in the late 1940s and early 1950s. In 1951, Forum member Commodore Cary W. Magruder (USN, RET) was elected to the commission with the avowed intent of making the commission more responsive to public needs. As commission chairman in 1953, he published the first administrative report, covering the years 1937 to 1952.

The Forum also urged that the governance of the ferry system and bridge be combined and turned over to the state. The state took over the bankrupt ferry system in 1951, but the bridge remained in the control of the commission until 1969 when the Newport Pell Bridge was opened.

JHS P2008.006.001

Anthony "Pat" Miller
Jamestown Superintendent of Schools.

Throughout the early 1950s, the organization held a series of well-attended public meetings on the competing financial demands of a new school and a sewage disposal facility. School Committee Chairman Fred C. Clarke and Superintendent Anthony J. Miller explained the school requirements to over 250 attendees at separate Forum meetings. A bond issue to build the Lawn Avenue School passed at the May 1953 Financial Town Meeting.

Advocacy for a sewage disposal plant was less successful, despite a state anti-pollution law passed in 1947. About 150 people listened to the heated discussion about how to fund such a plant, but no firm plan of action was proposed, and no wastewater treatment plant was built for over 25 years.

The Forum died a quiet death. The last newspaper account to mention the Forum appeared on June 22, 1955, and reported "meetings will be held at the call of the president or five members when matters vital to welfare of the community are to be discussed."

Most of the issues that the Forum attempted to enlighten the public about are no longer of concern. A charter that allows the hiring of a Town Administrator and of professionals for many of the jobs that in the past were elective passed in 1974; much of 1954 was spent discussing the pros and cons of this form of governance. Fort Getty was acquired for recreation despite some objections that the town didn't need a park that large. A permanent, trained police force replaced local constables in 1958.

Some issues still resonate. Recreational facilities were and are a concern. Traffic and parking and how to handle them warrant discussion. Introducing candidates to the electorate without reference to party affiliation is a biennial need.

A New Way to Run a Town

Until 48 years ago, Jamestown was run directly by its elected officials. The elected Town Council was expected to control the day-to-day operations of government. Much of the administrative responsibility fell to the Town Clerk, which was also an elective position.

A Town Charter, proposed in 1952, called for the employment of a Town Administrator to apply more professional methods to the business of the town. The 1952 charter was rejected, but the idea was resurrected 20 years later. The 1974 charter was approved by the voters by a margin of 3 to 2.

JHS P2001.095

Bob Sutton, Jamestown's First Town Administrator.

The first Town Administrator under the new charter was Robert W. Sutton Jr. Sutton had helped frame the charter, working as a full-time consultant to the Jamestown Charter Commission while employed by the Bureau of Government Research at URI. He accepted the job of interim Town Administrator on January 1, 1975, citing his philosophy that strong individual leadership should be combined with collaborative thinking to ensure an orderly establishment of the new administrative model.

In July, he accepted the job permanently and served for 17 years, the longest serving administrator to date. He was dedicated to maintaining the island's rural character and to a safe environment. His tenure saw the purchase of the golf course, an upgrade to the water treatment facility, and the building of the wastewater treatment plant as well as of a new police station and grammar school.

In 1992, Sutton left to work for the Rhode Island Department of Environmental Management. Sutton still lives in Jamestown and started Jamestown's Community Farm in 2000.

JHS P1994.028

The Jamestown Police Station. One of the major projects completed during Sutton's tenure as Town Administrator.

After a nation-wide search, the Town hired Frances H. Shocket from Cincinnati, Ohio, as the new Town Administrator in September 1992. Her first year was one of crisis. The Jamestown Verrazzano Bridge opened the day she took office. In the summer of 1993, water levels at the reservoir dropped to the lowest ever, and water had to be trucked in from North Kingstown. Traffic snarled everywhere as the John Eldred Parkway between the bridges was built.

JHS P2012.020.011

Fran Shocket.

Traffic eased with the opening of the parkway in 1994, but the water crisis continued to plague Shocket during her five years in office. She stepped down in December 1997 to become interim finance director for the city of Newport. The new job offered more money and less stress.

Maryanne Crawford, Town Administrator from 1998 to 2004, was promoted from within. She was a Jamestown resident and had been town Finance Director. Her strengths were in budgeting and financial management, and the decision to hire her was not unanimous. One council member stated that he felt the position needed more management training and experience.

In July 2004, Crawford left for an executive position with the East Greenwich school system. As one of her last acts, she informed the Town Council that the town had received notice of an improved, top financial rating, which would result in lower rates on bonds approved the previous November.

Mark Haddad.

Jamestown officials screened 40 job applicants before selecting Mark Haddad of Massachusetts as Town Administrator in late November 2004. Haddad had formerly been Town Manager in Cohasset but had resigned under a cloud of sexual harassment accusations. He lasted less than six months in Jamestown, resigning without giving a reason.

Early in 2005, the town welcomed a new Town Administrator, Bruce Keiser. Keiser had been a career government employee in Rhode Island since 1978 and said he came to Jamestown "to finish his career in tranquility." His nine years on the job were less than tranquil. Reflecting on his tenure in August 2013, Keiser recalled his first public meeting, a hearing about siting the highway barn at the landfill. "It was as raucous a public meeting I have ever attended," he said.

Keiser pointed to the farmland acquisition as one of his proudest moments, ignoring the completion of the new Town Hall and the final siting of the highway barn. "The ball was halfway down the road when I was hired," he said, "but I was lucky enough to bring it across the finish line."

Keiser's parting advice to the new administrator was "You're part of a team. Simple as that. You may be the point person, but it's a mutually respectful environment."

Courtesy of *The Jamestown Press*
Bruce Keiser.

The advice seems to have been lost on the next Town Administrator Keven Paicos, whose employment lasted only 147 days and ended bitterly. Formerly the Town Manager of Foxboro, Massachusetts, Paicos had often been in conflict with the Town Council there for his authoritarian management style. The disagreement in Jamestown was about the residency requirement and ended with the town paying an estimated $50,000 severance package.

A month after Paicos left, Jamestown had a new Town Administrator. Andrew Nota, who had been considered in the earlier search, had been South Kingstown's director of administrative services from 2009, and he had experience and first-hand knowledge of local conditions, particularly population changes, commercial fishing, and recreational programming – three major concerns of the Town Council.

Nota moved to Jamestown, solving the problem that had proved intractable with his predecessor. He immersed himself in the job, keeping an open-door policy in his office and closely tracking the day-to-day operations of town departments. In addition, he became vice president of the Rhode Island League of Cities and Towns, a membership organization of municipal-

Courtesy of *The Jamestown Press*
Andy Nota.

Courtesy of *The Jamestown Press*
Jamie Hainsworth.

ities that serves as the unified voice of local government in the Ocean State.

When Nota resigned in August 2019, he left an economically sound town with substantially improved recreational facilities and programs. The Town Council's search for a new administrator led them to a relatively new Jamestown resident, Jamie Hainsworth.

Hainsworth and his wife had moved to Jamestown in 2012 after he retired as Chief of Police of Gloucester, RI, in 2010. He then worked with Mothers Against Drunk Driving, as a victim's advocate. President Barack Obama appointed Hainsworth as U.S. marshal in June 2012, a position he held until ousted by the Trump administration in 2017. Hainsworth was sworn in as Jamestown's eighth chief executive in January 2020.

Courtesy of *The Jamestown Press*
Edward Mello.

When Hainsworth resigned in early 2023, the search for a new chief executive swiftly settled on Jamestown's own Chief of Police Edward Mello. Mello had come to Jamestown in 2011 from Westerly where he had been police chief for over six years and a member of the force for 23. He was appointed interim Town Adminstrator and took office on February 27.

Some Men of Jamestown

INTRODUCTION

Between 1800 and 1850, the population of Jamestown fell almost 30 percent. Young people, especially young men, left the island for a more attractive and lucrative future than raising sheep and subsistence farming offered. Those who went to sea, even when they continued to call Jamestown home, were absent for long periods. The surnames of many who remained were familiar and could be traced back to colonial times: Clarke, Carr, Weeden.

With the introduction of the steam ferry to Newport in 1873, newcomers came to the island. Some were from old Jamestown families, like the Caswells and the Peckhams, returning home. Others, such as the Brooks and Hunts, were attracted by the growing resort economy. The population of island almost tripled between 1870 and 1900.

The men who lived in Jamestown in the late 19th and early 20th centuries – whether they grew up here or moved here later – fueled the resort economy. Many of the native-born divided their family farms into building lots for the newcomers. They served on the board or managed the Jamestown & Newport Ferry Company, which was majority owned by the town. The newcomers opened new businesses, creating new jobs and expanded opportunities. Some old residents were lured back to their birthplace.

The men profiled in the following essays played roles or came from families that played roles in the transition of Jamestown from a simple farming village to a busy, prosperous town.

GUSTAVUS ADOLPHUS CLARKE

Gustavus Adolphus Clarke, known as G. Adolphus, was one of Jamestown's many descendants of Joseph Clarke, one of the original purchasers of Conanicut Island. He was born in Jamestown in 1839, eighth of the nine children of David Wright and Sarah Chaffee Clarke. He was in his mid-teens when his father died and his mother moved with the younger children to Newport.

Whatever plans the young G. Adolphus had for his future were interrupted by the onset of the American Civil War. Five days after Confederate guns around Charleston Harbor opened fire on Fort Sumter on April 12, 1861, he enlisted as a Private with Company F, 1st Regiment, R. I. Volunteers.

According to the historian of Company F, Charles H. Clarke, "Like the minute men of Revolutionary times, they left their bench, their desks, and farm, at the call to arms." The 1st Regiment left within the month for Washington, and on May 1, they paraded in front of the Patent Office while the Stars and Stripes was hoisted on the building by

Courtesy of Thought Co..

Ambrose E. Burnside, colonel, 1st Rhode Island Regiment.

149

President Lincoln. After the flag raising, the regiment was drilled by Colonel Ambrose Burnside under review by the President and members of the Cabinet. Almost immediately, the company set off for the front. In mid-July, they fought in the First Battle of Bull Run in Manassas, Virginia.

One story of Company F's activity in that battle evokes the total confusion and upset of the fog of war. "Shot and shell were flying in all directions; we had lost a number of men, and the other companies of the regiment had suffered considerable loss. An officer now rode in front of our regiment and gave the order to cease firing, as we were shooting our own troops. The smoke, which had occasioned this, soon lifted in our front, when we discovered a regiment bearing the union flag marching up the hill in our direction. When a short distance from us, they gave us a volley, which we returned at once, when they turned and retreated down the hill. This regiment was the 4th Alabama. . . . It was never known who the officer was that gave the order to cease firing."

Soon after the defeat at Bull Run, with their three-month term of enlistment completed and still of the opinion that the war would be won quickly, G. Adolphus Clarke and the rest of Company F returned home and were mustered out.

As the war continued, Clarke found a different way to express his patriotism. On August 6, 1862, Seaman's Protection Certificate #12 was issued to "Gustavius R. Clark," 22, of Jamestown by the Newport Customs Office. Under a 1796 law, customs collectors were directed to maintain a record of all United States citizens serving on United States vessels. These certificates vouched for the citizenship of the individual. After serving on a clipper ship for a trip around the Cape of Good Hope, Clarke enlisted in the navy, serving from February 1863 to March 1866.

On September 18, 1872, G. Adolphus married Hannah Carter Carr. Hannah was a descendant of Caleb Carr, another of Jamestown's first proprietors, and had grown up at the Carr family homestead on Carr Lane. Clarke became the purser on Jamestown's first steam ferry, *Jamestown*, which began service between Newport and Jamestown in 1873 and then sought appointment as a lighthouse keeper.

In the 18th and most of the 19th centuries, lighthouse keepers were political appointees. Although in 1852 the United States Light-House Board had issued rules about qualifications and conventional wisdom suggested that the best keepers were old sailors, political clout and military service still influenced appointments. Clarke, with his Civil War service and a brother who was superintendent of schools in Newport, had some of each and he was appointed keeper at Rose Island Lighthouse in 1879. The family lived on Rose Island until 1887.

Clarke's eight years on the island are notable for his conservation efforts. Rose Island was known as Conockono-

JHS P1981R.064d

Rose Island Lighthouse in 1889, two years after Clarke's tenure there.

quit by the Narragansett or "place of the long point." The long point was a grassy meadow at the northernmost point of the island. During his tenure on the island, Clarke pleaded with the authorities to protect the meadow with sea walls to prevent erosion, but his pleadings went unheeded. The great Portland gale of 1898 reduced the grassy cow pasture to the tidal flat that can be seen today only at low tide. Prior to the gale the island measured approximately 23 acres in size; today it measures only 18 acres, a loss of 5 acres.

G. Adolphus and Hannah Clarke had three children. Edith was born in 1873 and, as so often happened in the 19th century, did not survive her first year. Clarence was born in 1877 in Jamestown, and their third child, Celia Elizabeth, was born in January 1882 on Rose Island.

Clarke returned to Jamestown in 1887. He bought a house on Narragansett Avenue and opened a fish market. The market was probably seasonal, and for several years he also worked as a freight clerk for the Jamestown & Newport Ferry Company. He immersed himself in the life of the town and was one of the founding members of the Conanicut Grange in 1889.

He continued to take pride in his service in the Civil War and was an active member of the Company F Association. At the 1909 annual meeting and reunion of the association, he was one of 11 of the 19 surviving members of the unit present and was elected president for the ensuing year.

Clarke died in his Narragansett Avenue home on June 5, 1916. He was 77 years old.

THE BOWEN BROTHERS

George Wallin Bowen and his brother James Howard were born on the Point in Newport in 1882 and 1884, respectively. In their 20s, the two brothers went their separate ways – George to Chicago; J. Howard, as he was known, to the U.S. Navy. World War I interrupted George's plans. He joined the Merchant Marine, and both brothers served at sea during the war.

J. Howard retired from the Navy and came to Jamestown in the mid-1920s. Now in his early 40s, he began a new career as restaurateur and inn keeper. In 1928, he and his wife

JHS P2011.022.021

The Bowen Brothers, Howard and George, about 1935.

Irene bought the Harbor View Inn at 73 Conanicus Avenue, between the Bay View and the entrance to Shoreby Hill. The large house (which no longer exists) had been built by Abbott Chandler in 1897 to serve as a boarding-house for seamen. With the Bowens in charge, the

JHS P2004M.363

Harbor View, the Bowen's inn and restaurant on Conanicus Avenue.

inn was popular with single women, many of them teachers.

They had a restaurant in the inn, as well as The White Nook, a small seasonal eatery built by J. Howard in 1928 across the street on the waterside of Conanicus Avenue. Irene Bowen also held a victualing license for an establishment on Narragansett Avenue, probably in the Bay Shore Hotel, just west of the Bay View at 10 Narragansett.

The Bowens were among the first to apply for a liquor license after the repeal of Prohibition in 1933 and received the second license issued in James-town.

The country was in the grip of the Great Depression, and early in 1934, George Bowen with his wife Grace and teen-age daughter Geraldine

JHS P1968.034

The White Nook (left) and the Richardson's garage.

arrived from Chicago for "an extended stay" at the inn. They were soon followed by their son James Howard Bowen II and his young wife Maxine.

George was an organist and pianist, and he put those skills to work at once. Within the year, he was involved in musical events around the island. He directed minstrel shows at the Conanicut Grange and the Palace Theatre and led an orchestra that played for dances at the Holy Ghost Hall and for school graduations. He also took over the management of The White Nook, and Grace relieved Irene at the Bay Shore. Their son worked at both restaurants. It was truly a family affair.

J. Howard was undoubtedly grateful for the help. Shortly before his brother's arrival he had purchased the E.B. Brooks garage, which abutted the Harbor View on the south. Early in 1936, he decided to close the garage and convert the building to apartments. It is probable that he did most of the work himself, perhaps with the help of his students since he was a master carpenter and the manual training teacher at the Jamestown school. He completed the conversion before the 1938 Hurricane changed the face of the Jamestown waterfront forever.

JHS P1981S.007

The site of the White Nook after the 1938 Hurricane. Harbor View beyond.

Hurricane damage to Bowen's property was extensive. Although the newly renovated apartments escaped major harm, the porch and façade of the Harbor View Inn next door were severely damaged. The White Nook, on the waterside of the street, disappeared completely, along with much of the land on which it had stood.

Perhaps in an attempt to focus the town's attention on revitalizing the devastated waterfront, J. Howard, who had previously worked as the Town Assessor, ran for Town Council in the May 1939 election. He was elected Town Council President and held that position through most of the building of the Jamestown Bridge. He served only one term and was replaced by John L. Smith three months before the bridge opened in July 1940.

Early in 1940, while J. Howard was still Town Council President, the Bowens sold the Harbor View Inn. A year later, they bought the old Shoreby Hill Casino just north of the inn at the entrance to Shoreby Hill. They announced plans for extensive renovations, but once again a world war interfered. In September 1941, J. Howard was recalled. He served as a Chief Petty Officer in the U.S. Navy until April 21, 1945.

George returned to the Merchant Marine. During World War I, he has been a first mate; during the new conflict, he achieved his master's license, returning to Jamestown as Captain Bowen.

In the 1950s, both men retired to Florida, where George died in 1955. J. Howard continued to return to Jamestown each summer until his death in 1972.

THOMAS E. HUNT,
JAMESTOWN'S FIRST YEAR-ROUND DRUGGIST

In 1930, when Thomas E. Hunt first rented the store at the corner of Narragansett and Conanicus avenues, he was 46 years old and already a successful drugstore owner with two stores in Newport.

Hunt graduated from the Rhode Island College School of Pharmacy in 1904 and, after working for Caswell & Massey and Hall & Lyons in Newport, he opened his first store on Thames Street in March 1918. The *Newport Mercury* carried a long story about the opening, praising the furnishings, the layout, and the variety of goods. In addition to a very modern soda fountain, "wares include all kinds of soda waters, candles, pipes, cigars, cigarettes and tobaccos, stationery, patent medicines, medicinal supplies and accessories,

JHS P2007.009.012

The Hunt Block on Conanicus Avenue. Thomas Hunt's drugstore was in the unit at the far right.

157

with a special prescription department arranged to handle this important branch of trade with dispatch and precision."

Two years later, Hunt's wife Bessie died in the influenza epidemic leaving him with two pre-teen daughters. He remarried in October 1921. His new wife was a Jamestowner – Cathryn A. Freeman, whose father had been a bandleader at Fort Adams.

During the years following his marriage, Hunt expanded his Newport business, opening a second store on Touro Street in 1928 and serving on the Rhode Island State Board of Pharmacy under two Republican governors. Perhaps it was Cathryn who turned Hunt's attention to Jamestown. When Herbert F. Hammond renovated the old Caswell Block in 1929-1930, Hunt was his first tenant for the corner store.

For the next five years, the new store was a satellite to Hunt's Newport operations. It was only open in the summer, but it was run in a similar manner, featuring a soda fountain and all the goods customarily found in drugstores. Then, in 1934, the Hunts moved to Jamestown and from 1935 on the drugstore stayed open during the winter months.

Thomas Hunt quickly involved himself in Jamestown's political and social life. He became an active member of the Republican Town Committee – at the time, Jamestown voted two-to-one Republican. He was a charter member of the Jamestown Rotary, founded in 1941.

During World War II, both Hunts became part of the Civil Defense team. Cathryn, who had served in the U.S. Navy Disbursing Office & Supply Office in Newport during World

War I, joined the Jamestown Red Cross Ambulance and Rescue Motor Corps, organized in 1941. The service was the forerunner of today's EMS division. Thomas became chairman of Jamestown's Office of Civilian Defense and a member of the rationing board as well as the Red Cross.

When the war ended, Hunt turned his attention to more local issues. In 1944, he had purchased the entire block of stores that he had rented a unit in for almost 15 years. Three years later – just shy of his 63rd birthday – he retired and leased the property to L. Sanford Crowell. As a retiree, he had more time to devote to the business of the town.

From the time it was built in 1940 until the opening of the Newport Bridge in 1969, the Jamestown Bridge was operated by the Jamestown Bridge Commission; the members of the commission were elected by Jamestown voters. Hunt served

JHS P2001.081

Thomas Hunt (far right) was chairman of the Jamestown School Committee in 1952 during the planning for the Lawn Avenue School. Other members (left to right): Tom Sheehan, Fred Clarke Sr., Manuel Matoes, Helen Foley, and Mary O'Connor.

on the commission from 1948 to 1950; he was also a director of the Jamestown & Newport Ferry Company before the service was taken over by the state in 1951.

During the early 1950s, the post-war baby boom led to overcrowding of both the Thomas H. Clarke School, which stood where the library does now, and the Carr School on Clarke Street. Hunt served on the Jamestown School Committee throughout the long process of planning and building the Lawn Avenue School, which opened in 1955. He was School Committee chairman from 1952 through 1954.At the same time, he was a member of the original Board of Canvassers, established in 1951 when the permanent registration statute was first enacted.

Hunt remained active in Jamestown government into his 80s, although in later years, he became one of Jamestown's "snow birds," spending part of his winters in Florida where he died in 1965.

JHS P2019.200.711

His drugstore retained Hunt's name long after he was no longer associated with it.

THE CASWELL CLAN

There have been Caswells in Jamestown at least since the late 18th century, working their farms and making a living from the sea. The inventive and artistic creations of three of the members of the clan make them particularly fascinating.

Oliver Caswell: Deaf Mute Artist

Oliver Caswell was born in Jamestown about 1830 to a Jamestown ferry captain and his wife. He was a bright, inquisitive 3-year-old when he came down with scarlet fever. Scarlet fever is a bacterial infection related to strep throat that, when untreated, kills one in four people infected. It can now be controlled with antibiotics, but in the 19th century, scarlet fever epidemics killed many children, striking primarily those between the ages of 2 and 14.

Oliver's parents realized quickly that he could not hear, a not uncommon effect of scarlet fever. A few weeks later, he was totally blind. He could make sounds but could no longer form words.

When he recovered from the illness, he still had a child's desire to examine the world around him. He smelled everything he could lay his hands on. His father took the boy with him on the ferry, and he handled everything he could reach. He caressed dogs and cats. He called a bird to him with crumbs and touched and smelled it before letting it go. He

JHS A2019.1126.001

Oliver Caswell learning how to communicate.

would feel the lips of other people when they talked and then put his hand on his own.

He was also ungovernable and when thwarted became violent – braying, striking, and kicking violently. Communicating with him seemed impossible.

Schooling for the blind and deaf was in its infancy. The Perkins School for the Blind, the first school for the blind in the United States, was founded in Boston in 1829, and Oliver's worried parents took him there. Samuel Gridley Howe, the doctor who had founded the school, took an interest in the new student and engaged the help of Laura Bridgman, who was also deaf and blind, to help him teach the boy.

When Charles Dickens visited the school in 1842, he met Oliver and in his *American Notes* he tells the story of how the boy took his first steps toward communicating with those around him.

"Taking several articles having short names, such as key, cup, mug, &c., and with Laura for an auxiliary," Dr. Howe told Dickens, "I sat down, and taking his hand, placed it upon one of them, and then with my own, made the letters k-e-y. He felt my hands eagerly with both of his, and on my repeating the process, he evidently tried to imitate the motions of my fingers. In a few minutes he contrived to feel the motions of my fingers with one hand, and holding out the other he tried to imitate them, laughing most heartily when he succeeded."

Oliver quickly learned to imitate the doctor's motions, but it took many repetitions before he made the connection between the item he held and the letters he formed. The break-

JHS 2009.007.001, 2009.007.002, 2009.007.003

Three of the bead baskets that Oliver Caswell fashioned and sold to Jamestown tourists.

through moment came when Dr. Howe had him spell out bread, and Laura brought him a piece of bread. He smelled and tasted it and laughed out right as if to say "ah." By the end of the year, he had learned about 100 nouns.

Once communication had been established, Dr. Howe was able to teach Oliver to control his tendency to act out his anger. The young man learned to write, read Braille, and hone his talents as a wood worker. He kept a diary that reveals his engagement with everyday activities such as playing with a friend in the rain, eating pudding, and musing over the books he read.

When he left Perkins, Caswell came home to Jamestown to live with his parents. He was a local celebrity and helped support himself by making bead baskets that he sold to summer visitors. He enjoyed meeting people, and he could recognize by a handshake a person he had not met for several years.

He took great interest in learning about noted men, and when Dom Pedro, Emperor of Brazil, was in Newport, he sent for Caswell to visit him at his hotel. The emperor showed great interest in him, and at parting presented him with a ten-dollar gold piece.

Oliver Caswell died April 13, 1896.

John Robert Caswell: Peripatetic Inventor

John Robert Caswell, who was known as JR, was born in Somerset, MA, in 1875. He was only 22 and his bride, Isabella Collins, was 18 when they married. Soon after, the young couple moved to Jamestown, and over the next ten years, Isabella gave birth to six children.

In Jamestown, JR set himself up as a blacksmith. It was the beginning of the 20th century, and times were changing.

JHS P1987.012

JR Caswell (left) and Bowen von Schade on the bus that Caswell built to carry passengers between the East and West Passage ferries.

JR changed with them, morphing from blacksmith to machinist as cars replaced horses. He combined the two skills to build a bus to carry passengers between the East and West Passage ferries. He also constructed an acetylene gas generator in his shop on West Street to light the family's house around the corner on Columbia Avenue.

Radio fascinated him. The first commercial radio station KDKA out of Pittsburgh began broadcasting in 1920. According to family lore, JR built a radio receiver

JHS P2016.014.011

JR Caswell.

and rented Town Hall for a radio listening concert to give all Jamestown residents a taste of the new technology.

Isabella, too, contributed to the family income. Her grandson remembers her selling penny candy from the West Street building to the children on their way to the Carr School, which stood at the corner of West and Clarke streets.

Things fell apart in 1922. JR ran away with Kathryn Louise White, a Jamestown girl more than 30 years his junior. The couple traveled across Canada to the West Coast and then down to San Diego, where he worked as a machinist at Ryan Aircraft. Lindbergh's *Spirit of Saint Louis* was built at Ryan Aircraft, and JR told his grandchildren he worked on the plane.

In the meantime, back in Jamestown, Isabella was granted a divorce, and in 1927 she married widower Walter Bollons, a blacksmith and an employee of the Jamestown & Newport Ferry Company.

JR and Kathryn married in Louisiana in 1925. In the early 1930s, they settled in Nashville.

In Tennessee, JR worked for Betty Lou Bakery, and he entertained his children and grandchildren with stories of what happened there. The bakery made a birthday cake for Shirley Temple. The cake was seven feet tall and one of JR's tasks was to make aluminum supports and shelves to hold the cake steady while it was flown to California. Unfortunately, no one had considered the size of the loading door and the cake had to be tilted to fit through. The cake broke. But it was patched up and flown to Hollywood anyway.

JR's children from his first marriage visited him in Tennessee, and after about five years, JR, Kathryn and their three children returned to the island. The family continued to grow with three more children being born in Rhode Island.

Back home in Jamestown, JR continued his inventive ways.

At some point in his peripatetic career, he had worked in an electric motor factory and could rebuild electric motors and generators. One time he used varnished shoelaces to provide the necessary insulation.

The original water tower on Howland Avenue could overflow if too much water were pumped from the pumping station on Southwest Avenue. JR was working for the water company and constructed a float-operated semaphore that alerted the operator at the pumping station to shut the pump off.

In the 1930s, home heating oil was carried from the tanker truck to a home in 5-gallon cans and the cans were emptied through a large funnel into the oil tank. To speed up the process and make it less labor-intensive, JR used a discarded filling station gasoline pump with several gasoline pump hoses coupled together. He powered the pump with an automobile electric starter and the fuel truck's generator. The result was similar to the oil delivery trucks we see today.

John Robert Caswell died in June 1964 at 89 years of age.

"Babe" Caswell: Model Maker and Mariner

William Foster Caswell, John and Isabella's youngest child, was born in Jamestown in November 1909. Family lore says that "Babe" was his only name until he selected William Foster, an uncle's name, for himself when he started school. The story is given some credence from census records which state that at six months he had not yet been named.

Throughout his life, for day-to-day, he was called "Babe."

Like many men of his generation, Babe Caswell left school after the sixth grade. As soon as he was old enough, he apprenticed aboard the Merchant Marine ship *Annapolis* and then got a job as a fireman with the Jamestown & Newport Ferry Company. In 1930, he married Marion Albee, a telephone operator and, briefly, the editor of the short-lived weekly paper *The James-town Town Crier*, founded by Babe's older brother Ernest.

Babe Caswell in his stateroom in 1968.

About the same time as he joined the ferry company, Caswell discovered his love of model making. For his first attempt, he whit-tled and glued together a replica of an old sail-ing vessel. After build-ing several other models of old sailing ships, he turned to model aircraft. His first were powered by rubber bands. Later he built larger planes powered by gasoline engines. In a state-wide model competition, one of his planes, with a 6-foot wingspread, won two trophies and wood-carving kits.

Over more than 20 years, he carved models of ships, aircraft, and the ferryboats of Narragan-sett Bay.

Caswell rose quickly in the ferry company. As

Babe Caswell's model of the ferry-boat *Beaver Tail*.

fireman on the *Governor Carr*, he helped in the recovery of the beached ferry after the Hurricane of 1938 and is reputed to be the person who drove the cars off the recently stabilized ferryboat along a makeshift ramp. By the time he was 35, he was chief engineer.

Not all of Caswell's time was devoted to model-making or working. In 1943, he won a seat on the Town Council and was elected vice-president. In 1944 and 1945, he served as council president.

The combination of Caswell's political activities and maritime knowledge led to his appointment as manager of the ferry company. From its inception in 1873 until 1951 when it was leased to the state, the Jamestown & Newport Ferry Company was majority-owned by the Town of Jamestown, and the board of directors was elected by the voters of the town. Caswell became acting manager in late 1947. (He later complained that he worked for seven months as acting manager while receiving engineer's pay.) He was appointed manager in May 1948.

During Caswell's tenure, the purchase of the company's first diesel-powered ferry was negotiated. The abandonment of steam power was driven by economics. Projections estimated over 80 percent reduction in fuel cost with diesel power.

The *Gotham*, rechristened *Jamestown* (the company's third *Jamestown*), arrived in Narragansett Bay on January 16, 1950, after a rough 19-hour trip from the Chesapeake. The 22-year-old diesel-powered boat was sent to General Dynamics in New London for overhaul.

JHS P2013.007.009

The *Jamestown III,* the ferryboat that essentially ended Babe Caswell's career with the Jamestown ferries.

The new ferry was still not in operation by the Financial Town Meeting four months later. At the meeting, Jamestown voters rapped ferry operations in general and particularly the purchase of the still non-operational *Gotham*. Between purchase and repair, the *Gotham* cost the town about $250,000 and was instrumental in the transfer of the ferry system to state control in March 1951. Legal, political, and personal repercussions continued for years.

In November 1950, Caswell resigned. In his letter of resignation, he stated "I find it impossible to run the ferries often enough to satisfy the traveling public, economically enough to satisfy the taxpayers and at the same time pay the employees a decent living wage that they deserve and still keep the ferries up to the standards demanded by the Coast Guard inspection department. No business can be run successfully without enough capital to back it. This the ferry company has never had."

After his resignation, Caswell returned to the sea as a Merchant Marine. He and his wife continued to live in Jamestown. Although he served on the Jamestown Bridge Commission for a while, he seems to have taken little further interest in Jamestown political life – maritime or otherwise.

Marion Caswell died in 1965 and Babe retired from the sea in 1971. He died on his 80th birthday at his daughter's home in Flint, Michigan.

THE PECKHAMS: FATHER AND SON

John Peckham, a Newport freeholder, was one of Jamestown's first landowners. Although he was not one of the 101 signers the Conanicut Island prepurchase agreement, his name appears on Joshua Fisher's 1658 map of the island. Over the years, the family maintained its connection to Jamestown, and John's many times great-grandson Alvin Peckham moved to Jamestown soon after his marriage in 1880.

Alvin was a farmer who, like many Jamestown farmers, discovered that supporting the burgeoning resort economy was more lucrative than farming. He founded a hauling business and brought in much of the raw materials needed to build the cottages and hotels of the resort era.

The family lived where the business demanded. Peckham first leased the Howland farm, near the center of the island and then moved to the Cottrell farm, south of and closer to the ferries. Later he built a home on Howland Avenue, near the lumber yard and mill that he and Louis Anthony set up in 1903. It was Jamestown's first lumber mill, and the two men brought the lumber from their woodland in Canaan, New Hampshire. He even tried his hand at being a developer himself, building "Harmony Villa" on Union Street.

A staunch Republican, he served on the Town Council and was a director of the Jamestown & Newport Ferry Company. He died at the age of 48 in March 1914.

The Peckham's only son, Preston Everett Peckham, born in 1884, proved to be one of Jamestown's most colorful turn-of-the-century characters. He was only 16 when he imported 25 pairs of homing pigeons from Belgium. The following year one of his pigeons came in second, by one minute, in a 10-hour race from Saybrook to Jamestown.

The tall, slender, brown-eyed, black-haired Preston – the description is from his World War I draft card – was evidently energetic and full of fun. In July 1903, the *Newport Daily News* reported "Things being dull about the wharf Tuesday, the drivers of the public carriages organized a carriage parade . . . led by Mr. Preston Peckham." He led the vehicles that were

JHS P1982.089

Preston E. Peckham and his wife Catherine taking a chilly winter carriage ride.

Horses Bought and Sold on Commission

PRESTON E. PECKHAM
HORSES
For Sale, Exchange and To Let

Jamestown, R. I. Dec 22 1915

waiting at the ferry wharf for passengers and freight along the front of Shoreby Hill and then up and through the recently platted Shoreby roads. "The carriages made a very credible appearance and no doubt increase of business will result from the parade," the *News* continued.

That was the first mention of Peckham's continuing involvement with horses. By 1910, married to Catherine Donohue and with a one-year-old daughter to support, he was managing his own horse livery. The livery leased out horses for riding and for draft during this period of transition from animal-drawn to automotive transport. Later, as draft animals became less in demand, his business included other farm animals and livestock.

His main love, however, was his horses. He organized horse and buggy races on Beavertail. The races were popular. About 300 people lined Beavertail Road one Monday afternoon in October 1928 to watch. The first two races pitted two horses against each other. Preston drove his own "Lady Rawlinson" to victory in the first. The second was won by Alvin Peckham, driving "Joe." In the last race, the free-for-all, all four horses were entered. In a close contest "Indian Girl," which "Lady Rawlinson" had beaten in the first race, won. So the matter of supremacy remained unsettled, though a future race was promised.

At his livery, Peckham conducted a riding academy for summer visitors, and in 1929 he began importing saddle horses from North Dakota to use at the school and to sell to other riding academies in southern New England. During one such transfer, two of the horses escaped and had to be rounded up by the state police. The resulting publicity may have boosted sales since several of the animals were sold before they reached the Jamestown ferry.

Throughout his life, Peckham was also involved in the business of the town. Each year from 1924 to 1930, he was elected Town Clerk on the Democratic Party ticket. He was also, at different times, a member of the Town Council, Chairman of the Board of Tax Assessors, director of public welfare, and a member of the board of directors of the Jamestown & Newport Ferry Company, serving for years as its secretary.

Preston E. Peckham died on Sunday, April 20, 1947.

THREE COUSINS

Thirteen Jamestown men died in service during World War II: Everett Alward, Howard Arnold, Bernard Anthony Brooks, Charles Brooks Jr., Lewis Burdick, Damon Cummings, Arthur Day, Delbert Gravatt, Frank Leighton, David Masterson, William H. Sweet, James Williams, and Francis X. Zweir. A heavy toll for a small town of fewer than 1800 inhabitants.

The hardest hit family was the Brooks. Three first cousins – Charles Brooks Jr., Bernard Anthony Brooks, and William C. Sweet – died.

William Brooks, the patriarch of the Brooks clan, was chief engineer on the Jamestown and Newport ferries from 1896 to 1918. He and his wife Sarah brought up their eight children in Jamestown and most of them continued to live in the town as adults.

Charles H. Brooks Jr. was the only son of William and Sarah's third son, Charles. Charles Sr. was the manager of the Jamestown & Newport Ferry Company in the 1920s and 1930s. He oversaw the construction of the Jamestown Bridge and was manager of the bridge during World War II.

Charles Jr. joined the Merchant Marine soon after graduating from Rogers High School. He worked for the American Export Line for several years in the late 1920s and in the depths of the Great Depression was one of the many James-

JHS P1973.028

Jamestown's Clarke School graduating class of 1927 with their teachers (back row). Charles Brooks Jr. is the fifth boy from the left.

towners employed at the Naval Torpedo Station. In 1937 he returned to the sea as assistant engineer on George F. Woolworth's yacht *Viking* for a South American and European cruise. He was then rehired by the American Export Line.

Early in the war, the Merchant Marine was incorporated as a branch of the military forces. Charles Jr. became a Lieutenant Commander serving in the Pacific. In March 1945, he went ashore in the Philippines with a hunting party. The group was ambushed, and he was shot by a Japanese sniper. His only child, Susan, was four months old when her father died.

Bernard Anthony Brooks was the only son of Charles Sr.'s younger brother Edward, the founder of the E.B. Brooks Oil Company. He was born and grew up in Jamestown and worked for a while for his father's oil distribution company.

For about two years, he, like his cousin, served in the Merchant Marine as a junior engineer.

At the time of his death, Bernard was a Naval Reserve fireman, first class, on the mine-sweeper *Eagle*. He had recently become engaged to be married. He was home in Jamestown and

JHS P2004M.131
The house at 121 Conanicus Avenue where Bernard Brooks grew up.

his automobile struck a culvert and telephone pole on East Shore Road. He died in November 1941, a few weeks before Pearl Harbor.

William H. Sweet was the son of the baby of the Brooks family, Cornelia, and her husband William C. Sweet. Twelve years younger than her brothers Charles and Edward, who were only 13 months apart, Cornelia was still in her teens when their father died.

Her two sons, William and David, were born in James-town, but the family moved to Newport while William was still in grade school. William enlisted in the Army Air Force four months after graduating from Rogers High School in 1942 and initially was in training to serve on C-47 military transport planes. He asked for and received reassignment to bombers. After training as an engineer, he was sent by way of North Africa to Italy in July 1944, where his crew joined the 513th Squadron of the 376th Bombardment Group (Heavy), flying 4-engine long-range B-24 Liberator bombers.

Courtesy of Lockheed Martin, Co.

A B-24 Liberator bomber like the one that William Sweet flew in World War II.

The crew had already flown 17 missions when, on September 10, 1944, they took off to bomb an ordnance plant in Vienna, Austria.

According to the bombardier on the mission, "The Vienna flak was heavy, intense, and accurate." It ripped a gaping hole in the right wing and punctured a gas tank. Other flak damaged the left wing. Flying home, with gasoline leaking from holes in the wings and a damaged fuel distribution system, they ran out of fuel halfway across the Adriatic Sea.

All ten crew members parachuted into the sea. William, who as engineer was responsible for the proper operation of the engines, was the next to last to leave the plane and thus was one of the farthest down the ten-mile path that the plane traveled during the evacuation.

Most of the crew were picked up by an Italian fishing boat. Only William Sweet and the ball turret gunner were not found in the rough sea.

Bibliography

Anonymous. "Growth of Jamestown. Developing a Watering Place." *Newport Journal* (September 13, 1902).

Enright, Rosemary and Sue Maden. "Brooks family lost three members during World War II." *The Jamestown Press* (January 12, 2023).

___ "Caswell played several key roles in final years of town-owned ferry." *The Jamestown Press* (July 21, 2022).

___ "Chamber predecessor targeted tourism to ease downturn." *The Jamestown Press* (September 22, 2022).

___ "Civil War veteran spent postwar career as Rose Island light keeper." *The Jamestown Press* (October 8, 2020).

___ "Clarke family women have had big impact on town." *The Jamestown Press* (March 19, 2020).

___ "Conanicut Battery has long served the island." *The Jamestown Press* (June 1, 2017).

___ "Cottrell Farm widow fights vices." *The Jamestown Press* (September 23, 2021).

___ "Former Walcott lady lent a hand to Belgium in war." *The Jamestown Press* (April 16, 2020).

___ "History of town administrators has been hit and miss." *The Jamestown Press* (September 15, 2019).

___ "How Pierce Avenue got its name." *The Jamestown Press* (March 26, 2015).

___ "J. R. Caswell was an inventive contributor to town." *The Jamestown Press* (April 14, 2022).

___ "Jamestown Forum was influential for a brief period." *The Jamestown Press* (June 23, 2022).

___ "Jamestown Rotary: Service above self." *The Jamestown Press* (March 10, 2016).

___ "Local women leave mark on postmaster position." *The Jamestown Press* (March 10, 2022).

___"Marsh madness: Gardeners save the salt marsh." *The James-town Press* (March 30, 2017).

___"Narragansett Avenue or Ferry Road?." *The Jamestown Press* (April 23, 2015).

___"Peckham men from farmers to ferryboats." *The Jamestown Press* (December 22, 2022).

___"Pharmacy owner Hunt wore many hats during his time." *The Jamestown Press* (April 25, 2019).

___"Scarlet fever victim left mark on Dickens, found friendship with Brazil's emperor." *The Jamestown Press* (December 12, 2019).

___"Sibling restaurateurs see action in both world wars." *The James-town Press* (January 21, 2021).

___"Southern belle makes way from Bayou to Beavertail." *The Jamestown Press* (June 25, 2020).

___"Street names and their stories." *The Jamestown Press* (April 19, 2018).

___"Street names share family history with families." *The James-town Press* (July 23, 2020).

___"Tennant sisters' lives were enlivened by disappearance of Dutch husband." *The Jamestown Press* (September 10, 2020).

___"The man whose name provided us with Avenue B." *The James-town Press* (February 14, 2019).

___"Windmill stewards establish local historical society." *The Jamestown Press* (August 19, 2021).

Tallman, Mariana M. *Pleasant Places in Rhode Island, and How to Reach Them.* Providence: The Providence Journal Company, 1893. Pp 56-62.

Watson, Walter Leon. "A Trip Around Jamestown," unpublished, 1928. (Typescript available at the Jamestown Historical Society, Object ID A2006.402.003).

Index

About the Authors

Rosemary Enright holds a BA and an MA in English (Rosary Hill College, 1962; New York University, 1963) and has completed extensive graduate work in American civilization at New York University. Her professional careers include editorial work, teaching English at New York Institute of Technology, freelance writing, and work as a process engineer and computer systems requirement analyst for Northrop Grumman Corporation. She has been active in the Jamestown Historical Society since 2002, serving as an officer and a director. She is currently treasurer and editor of the biennial newsletter.

Sue Maden attended Carleton College (1952–54) and then studied nursing (BS in nursing, Cornell University– New York Hospital School of Nursing, 1957; MA in public health nursing, Hunter College, 1963). After a variety of nursing positions, she earned a master's in library science at Pratt Institute (1974) and subsequently worked at the Columbia University Health Science Library. Retiring to Jamestown in 1982, she has since focused on volunteer work and local history projects. She has served several terms on the board of the Jamestown Historical Society, and currently is vice-president and chair of the Exhibit and Print Media committees.

Together with Peter Fay, Sue and Rosemary contribute monthly Jamestown history articles to *The Jamestown Press*.

Other Books by the Authors

Enright, Rosemary. *A Dictionary of Rhode Island Biography, 1636-1800.* Providence, RI: Rhode Island Library Association, 1976.

——. *50 Original Sketches* (South County Authors). Providence, RI: Rhode Island Library Association, 1979.

Maden, Sue. *Greetings from Jamestown, Rhode Island: Picture Post Card Views, 1900-1950.* Jamestown: West Ferry Press, 1988.

——. *The Jamestown Bridge, 1940-1990: from "The Bridge to Nowhere" to Obsolescence.* Jamestown, RI: Jamestown Historical Society, 1990.

Maden, Sue and Patrick Hodgkin. *Jamestown Affairs: A Miscellany of Historical Flashbacks.* Jamestown: West Ferry Press, 1996. (Collected essays)

Maden, Sue with Dick Allphin and Tom McCandless. *The Building Boom in Jamestown, Rhode Island, 1926-1931.* Jamestown: West Ferry Press, 2004.

Maden, Sue. *The Jamestown Bridge, 1940-2007: Concept to Demolition.* Jamestown, RI: Jamestown Historical Society, 2007.

Enright, Rosemary and Sue Maden. *Jamestown: A History of Narragansett Bay's Island Town.* Charelston, SC: The History Press, 2010.

——. *Legenary Locals of Jamestown.* Charelston, SC: Arcadia Publishing, 2014.

——. *Historic Tales of Jamestown.* Charelston, SC: The History Press, 2016. (Collected essays)

Maden, Sue with Rosemary Enright. *The Diary of Providence Reform School Inmate No. 2067: Dr. William Lincoln Bates, 1855-1932.* Jamestown, RI: Jamestown Historical Society, 2019.

Made in USA - North Chelmsford, MA
1363295_9798378330126
03.25.2023 1336